THE CHRISTIAN AND WORLD
INTEGRATION

IS VOLUME

95

OF THE

Twentieth Century Encyclopedia of Catholicism

UNDER SECTION

IX

THE CHURCH AND THE MODERN WORLD

IT IS ALSO THE

103RD

VOLUME IN ORDER OF PUBLICATION

Edited by HENRI DANIEL-ROPS of the Académie Française

THE CHRISTIAN AND WORLD INTEGRATION

By *JACQUES LECLERCQ*

Translated from the French by P. J. HEPBURNE-SCOTT

19526

HAWTHORN BOOKS · PUBLISHERS · *New York*

First Edition, April, 1963

NIHIL OBSTAT

Daniel Duivesteijn, S.T.D.

Censor Deputatus

IMPRIMATUR

Georgius L. Craven

Episcopus Sebastopolis, Vic. Cap.

Westmonasterii, die XXXI JANUARII MCMLXIII

H-9533

CONTENTS

CHAPTER I

INTERNATIONAL INTEGRATION

Before speaking of the Christian attitude we must first review the needs of the times, which arise from the circumstances in which men live, for the Christian is in the world, must take his place in the world, must act on the world, and he will not do this with any success unless he accepts the world as it is.

Now the world will not last for ever, which means first of all that it changes. To say that the world will not last for ever does not mean only that it will come to an end, which has little interest for us, provided that we come to an end beforehand. It also means that the world changes, that the world of today is not the world of yesterday. Now it is in the world of today that we live; it is in the world of today that we ought to live.

This last statement may seem a trifle superfluous, for of necessity we live in the world of today; we do not know how to do otherwise, and in any case we have no choice. But we can refuse to accept the world as it is, refuse to take it into consideration, insist on living as if the world were the same as it was a hundred years ago, systematically condemn all that is new, refuse to take any notice of it. And side by side with those who do not want to see what has changed, are those who, for various reasons, are un-aware of what is happening. We shall have to analyse some of these cases. At any rate, if we are to live fully in the world of our time, we must be aware of what our time is, what it brings, what it needs, what it forbids. Therefore, as we are dealing with international integration, we must first look this fact squarely in the face.

HOW DOES INTERNATIONAL INTEGRATION ARISE?

International integration arises in the first place from the development of communications. It began with the discovery of steam and continued with the discovery of electricity. The steam engine, the railway, the steamboat, then telegraphy and the telephone brought men closer together. However, in the twentieth century this drawing together was hastened by the aeroplane and the radio which enabled the farthest corners of the earth to com-municate with each other within a few hours; and the rapidity of movement continues to increase.

However, communications are only a result. They are related to all technical and scientific development, for the characteristic of technical development in our day and age is that it is an application of scientific development. It was not so in former times; technical developments in past centuries were brought about empirically, one might almost say instinctively, simply by noting that the best results could be obtained by such and such a procedure. Nowadays technological process is deliberate; we seek it and to that end we organize research. Pure science is placed at the service of applied science. Science and technology go together, and it is this combination which leads to the international integration of human activity.

To understand the closeness of this combination we

need only to analyse the factors making up one of the means of communication which enables men, merchandise, pictures or voices to be transported across the world. Take the aeroplane, for example. It cannot be isolated from scientific progress or from the whole mass of the technical applications of science. In its manufacture many metals are used which hitherto could not be worked in the way necessary for making aircraft; materials of all types are incorporated; the aeroplane is also dependent on the science of engines, both the construction of engines and the fuel used in them; yet again it utilizes signalling systems to enable it to communicate at long distances; and there are many other aspects of science and technology involved.

WHAT IS INTERNATIONAL INTEGRATION?

International integration is the fact that the activities of the entire human race form a whole. Chinese physicists, working in America and receiving a Nobel Prize awarded by the Stockholm Academy, are a good example of international integration; it is a collaboration of Asia, America and Europe. The whole world is involved.

The example just quoted concerns science. In the field of conjugal relationship, the Ogino-Knaus method is often spoken of: Ogino is a Japanese scholar and Knaus is Dutch. Simply the association of these two names indicates the fact of international integration. Moreover, the Ogino-Knaus method is spoken of in every country of the world, and the majority of people do not know what the nationalities of the bearers of these two names are. We do not think of it; the method forms a part of the universal patrimony of the human race.

What is true of science is also true of the mind. When Aldous Huxley, an English writer living in America, describes in one of his novels an American who takes up Buddhist contemplative exercises, and when Gandhi and Tagore pay tribute to Christianity for giving them ideas which enabled them to guide the Hindu tradition into new paths; when Chinese communists apply the theories of Karl Marx, a German Jew who wrote in England, they all bear witness to the fact that henceforth the thought and aspirations of the human race are adapted to an international level. We no longer find ourselves faced with a Christianity enclosed within itself, an Islam enclosed within itself, a Chinese or a Hindu tradition enclosed within itself; we are faced with a united world in which various ideologies are present, but where all of them are present everywhere.

About the Algerian situation, many French people were pained because the subject was not confined exclusively to France, and because the whole world took an interest in it; and during the Spanish civil war, when Franco's troops, who considered themselves "crusaders", committed the same atrocities as the republican troops, a Swedish newspaper wrote: "For some time past we have felt sympathetic towards Catholicism, but if this is Catholicism our sympathy is dead!" A weekly paper in India expressed the same idea. And when, again in Spain, the Protestants complain of persecution, the United States of America intervenes.

In the United States of America itself, when unrepentant segregationists assaulted the negroes, President Eisenhower declared: "These segregationists are ruining the influence of the United States in the world."

Need we go on? The instances are innumerable. When the Russians crushed the revolution in Budapest, no more than two hours later there were demonstrations in front of Soviet embassies at the other side of the world. To appreciate the difference between the different eras, consider these few instances: when Poland rebelled in

1831, the Russians quietly crushed the insurrection and it was all over before anything was heard of it abroad. This was the origin of the famous saying of General Sebastiani in the French parliament: "Order is restored in Warsaw." The Russians had massacred them all. Certainly, many Westerners were disillusioned that no one intervened more forcefully in Budapest, but can we believe that the Kremlin was indifferent to the fact that each of its actions was attended by worldwide outcries, or that India, with whom it enjoyed good relations, demanded that a commission of inquiry be sent out?

I have not mentioned here the politico-economic aspect of the question, because that is generally discussed, and my readers are well aware of it. Everyone knows that the oil problem is a worldwide problem, as is the problem of hunger. When newspapers daily denounce the scandalous fact that 20 per cent of the human race controls 80 per cent of the world's resources, they state in effect that humanity forms a whole and that we have passed the stage where a citizen had only to concern himself with the welfare of his city. We have arrived at the stage where each man must concern himself with all men. When there are threats of war, the whole world feels itself threatened.

THE MORAL REQUIREMENTS OF INTERNATIONAL INTEGRATION

It is self-evident that international integration is the unity of the human race, not in the sense that all men should have the same nature, but in the sense that all men have an effect on each other throughout the whole world. But if they affect each other, then they ought to coordinate their actions, or this mutual reaction will end in fighting, as often happens. I shall speak of this later.

International integration implies coordination. and this

coordination must be on an international scale. Generally speaking, when men have a common interest, they should group themselves together in order to promote it, and there must be human and social groups at every level where there are common interests. If the inhabitants of a city, or a district, or a country, have interests in common, they should take communal action, and this should spring from a community spirit at the level of the city, or the district, or the country. If all the inhabitants of the world have interests in common, they should promote a community spirit at world level.

International integration means that the world forms a community. There should therefore be a community spirit, and community spirit means that each one concerns himself with the common welfare.

The majority of us would be hard put to it to define this common welfare. Much has been written about it at the national level, under the titles of civic duty and patriotism. Love of one's country is what unites a nation, for example; but what is one's country? We know how unhelpful patriotic literature is to those who want a definition pretending to any degree of exactitude. People may have the most conflicting ideas of what constitutes the good of their country, they may support opposing forms of government, belong to different religions, speak different languages, uphold different moralities; all of them agree that their country is not any or all of these things, yet the nation as a whole forms an indestructible community.

It is no different at the international level. International integration implies a sense of community corresponding to the mass of reasons which bring men together. We have just reviewed these reasons. If international integration is to bring about the happiness of the human community, in accordance with what is allowed by the civilization of the time, there must develop a feeling of solidarity which will extend throughout the world.

We know, for example, that in national communities, a sense of the common good has been developed which entails the sacrifice of personal interests when these are contrary to the common good in certain circumstances. We have, for example, arrived at the stage where war does not enter into national conflicts. Sometimes the threat of war is used, but practically speaking it is inconceivable that a party or a district in a country would deliberately commence military operations against the rest of the country or against another district or another party, as did the satraps in the former Persian Empire, or the feudal lords of the Middle Ages. In the same way, no district would demand to be separated from the rest of the country on the grounds that unity was a disadvantage to it.

In the same way famine is now unheard of in our countries, because each country forms an entity, and if famine threatens one region, the whole country takes the necessary steps to prevent it. On a world scale, the same solidarity is now necessary and possible. On all sides we hear of catastrophes which will occur if this solidarity is not created. But awareness follows slowly on the heels of fact. International integration does not affect hearts as quickly as it affects life, and so we find that human progress is disjointed.

The lack of balance is obvious, but we must analyse its causes and study its effects if we are to specify what Christians can and should do.

THE OBSTACLES

We live in the era of the aeroplane, that much is evident, but to what extent does the aeroplane have an effect on life? To what extent do people react to the pace set by the aeroplane?

Airline companies, anxious for publicity, tell us of the number of travellers they carry. Their numbers run into millions. But it cannot be said that these millions represent men; because they merely express millions of journeys. Some men travel by air fifty times a year.

It would be interesting to estimate the number of English or American people who have already travelled by air, the number who travel by air at least once a year, the number who fly regularly. No statistics are available on this point. They would cost a lot of money to compile and no one would spend this money on it because there is no financial gain to be made. However, they would be enlightening for anyone seeking to learn to what extent the aeroplane influences present-day life.

We ought also to find out how many of these people travel by air, not only to places outside their own country, but to other continents. Even without the necessary statistics I am prepared to say that the vast majority of people never use an aeroplane.

It is true that the aeroplane affects us indirectly. We see them in the sky; the aeroplane now forms an integral part of the skyscape; the newspapers speak of them; they can be seen at the cinema and in the illustrated magazines. We are accustomed to live in a world of which the aeroplane is a part. But what repercussions has this phenomenon produced with regard to international affairs?

We have already mentioned the worldwide reactions to the internal affairs of different countries; but are not these reactions the work of a very few people? If a thousand people demonstrate in front of a Soviet embassy, in a capital containing millions of inhabitants, does it mean that the population as a whole is profoundly moved by the event? When the segregationists of Little Rock demonstrate against the admission of coloured students into schools hitherto reserved for whites, they are to all intents and purposes thinking only of themselves and their local traditions. Their horizon is limited to Little Rock. Certainly, the President of the United States sees further, but how many Americans see the repercussions in Africa, arising from the conditions in which the negroes in their town or neighbourhood live, as a decisive factor in the question? To coin a phrase of present-day philosophy we could ask: How many Americans consider that the international implications of the colour question with which they are faced are of essential importance? How many see them as an integral part of our life, as opposed to abstract facts of purely academic interest which have no direct influence on life?

The traveller notices this. When one travels abroad and mixes with the people of another country, it always happens that, as soon as the first polite exchanges have been made, the conversation turns to local affairs, to the life of the neighbourhood; and this local life is dominated by those— the vast majority—who never travel. In some gatherings of important men, who form, furthermore, only a small proportion of the population, the conversation may reach as high as national interests. But what of the world? What of the famine in India and South America? How much is said of cooperation between peoples?

One of the places in the world where it would be interesting to study these levels of interest would undoubtedly be Paris, for Paris is one of the most cosmopolitan cities in the universe, and it is also one of the cities on which the eyes of the universe are most often fixed. There are few cities where one can encounter more people from every nation, some staying for long periods, others passing through, intellectuals, professors, artists, students, politicians, business men. American illustrated magazines devote an article nearly every week to Paris, or to some aspect of Paris. In theory it would be logical to expect the

Parisian to be intensely interested in world affairs; but when one arrives in Paris one is astonished to find that the Parisian thinks only of Paris, and that, as far as he is concerned, the communal life of men is reduced to what goes on in Paris. If he questions a foreigner about what is happening in his native land it is only to find out what people are thinking about Paris, or, at the most, of France—though, for the Parisian, France is still Paris. The problems facing other countries, those problems facing the world, which do not concern Paris, do not interest him, and if the foreigner begins to speak of them, instead of questioning him eagerly, he will turn the conversation.

I am speaking here of Paris because it is a capital city known to very many outside it, both in Europe and other countries; but the same phenomenon can be seen everywhere. It is exactly the same in London, New York or Little Rock. How are we to make mankind lift itself up to view the vast perspective of civilization?

Our Western countries have done the most to integrate fully our present-day civilization; they are the authors of it, and it is due to their efforts that it has progressed this far. What can be said, then, of the millions of men who live in Asia, in Africa, in South America, the uneducated—or the illiterate as we call them today—the underfed, the badly housed and wretchedly clothed, confined to their birthplace, and to the traditions and customs which they find there?

It is not enough to collect facts; we must explain them. The obstacles can be divided into two kinds, psychological and moral.

We can take the psychological obstacles first. Man is not very intelligent. He is undoubtedly gifted with intelligence. This is what gives him his dignity; this is the source of civilization. However, his intelligence is slow and clumsy.

When faced with a new idea he absorbs it with difficulty. For this reason his life is governed by habit, habits of mind and habits of action. Man likes to do as he has always done, to think as he has always thought, to say what he has always said. When something new arises, he tries to fit it into his pattern of habits.

Now we live in an age when life has been severely upset, and is being still more upset every day. Our minds resist any too rapid advance of facts, and thus man lags behind his own progress.

How is this possible, since progress comes from him? Here again we are faced with a paradox. Progress springs not from mankind as a whole, but from a small number of men. Nuclear fission, antibiotics and computers are the result of work done by a small number of research workers, although they are afterwards used by the masses. Moreover, these inventions are split up into various spheres, some in one field of research, some in another, without any apparent connection; even those who have made a discovery are, in so far as general ideas and conceptions of life are concerned, as retarded as the rest. They are specialists who work in one narrow sphere; but, when all these individual discoveries are multiplied, intensified and circulated to any great extent, they necessitate a transformation of the whole of life itself, of the general conceptions of life, and, in certain fields at least, of the general outlook on the world; and this transformation is not brought about by the specialists themselves; they merely launch their own individual inventions. Others must then intervene to modify the conceptions of life; but must not these others be rather more than human?

This is the problem which now faces us. The fact of international integration calls for the international integration of thought, but thought is slow to change. Doubtless, in the field of thought there is a small number of men who correspond to the inventors in the technical field, but the majority are more prone to accept material devices which offer them facilities or pleasure than to reflect on problems of conduct. Those who travel by air do so in their own interests, which are the same as they have always been— for example, they want to enjoy themselves, to see beautiful scenery, to make money, etc.—they use this technical discovery without any alteration in their outlook, and take their old soul on to new beaches. Those who follow world events on the cinema screen are only superficially interested, and keep in their hearts their preoccupation with their personal lives.

There is therefore a psychological obstacle preventing our understanding the necessity for a reorientation of human conduct. Attempts have been made by various organizations, such as Unesco, schools and youth movements, to overcome this obstacle by international meetings and by exchanges of children between various countries. But all this is extremely slow, and usually affects only a small number. I have said before that only a few are directly affected by the aeroplane and by radio; those who are affected by the idea of a world community are scarcely more numerous, and, moreover, they are not the same people as those affected by modern means of communication.

For example, a person may hear on the radio news about the world as a whole, and yet still remain preoccupied, in his personal life, with his own interests. I mean by that, with the immediate interests of his daily life, the only interests that he is accustomed to take into consideration. For it is evident that it is in his own interests that the whole of his country should not be blown sky-high by a few of those bombs which are daily being still further perfected. But this is not something which he experiences in his daily life, like the prompt arrival of the 'bus he travels on each morning, or the electric lighting of his house. It can be clearly seen at election time, in every country, that it is home policy, and quite often local policy, which is the deciding factor in elections. If this is the case in the most highly developed countries, how much more so is it in Transjordan or Burma?

However, there are two parts to this problem. First, there is the movement of public opinion, which is clearly seen in any group of people. It is obvious to the Americans or to the English, for example, that the national community should ensure certain conditions of life for the whole of the population, such as keeping the peace. If, in one town, the people start to massacre each other, troops are sent to restore order. The whole community pays the cost, and no one complains about it. We must begin to form a similar climate of opinion at the international level. When this is achieved many positive measures, that no one would dare even to suggest at the moment, would be considered as a matter of course.

Secondly, the problem concerns the economic, cultural and political leaders. They are the tributaries of public opinion, which approves some actions, puts up with others and reacts against still others. The leaders who have to make decisions are themselves part of the public and share its attitude of mind. The politician has not necessarily a more open mind than the man in the street. More often than not he is the man in the street, and it is because the man in the street has a fellow feeling for him that he trusts him. But if we are to create a united Europe to start with, and a united world to go on with, it must be the politicians who lead the way.

They will not do so without coming under pressure, under economic and cultural pressure for example. To take only the economic aspect, industrialists and business men, preoccupied with their immediate interests, will seek to guarantee their protection, as far as they can do so without exciting public opinion against them. At conferences many praiseworthy principles may be proclaimed; in the practical atmosphere of daily life each industrialist and business man is engrossed in his own affairs, in the immediate interests of his own affairs, in what can, at this moment, help his own affairs to prosper. Even when Europe was united to the extent of a treaty being signed to do away with customs barriers, certain countries immediately took steps to reinforce these barriers against the entry of certain products, because of pressure from interested parties, absorbed in their own immediate concerns.

If we are to counteract this, we must so form public opinion that certain measures will become impossible. It always comes back to public opinion, to the attitude of the majority. This majority is extremely slow to change its outlook. It does not understand a great deal. When it thinks it understands it has often got hold of the wrong end of the stick. It does not grasp a problem in its entirety, and often cribs at minor wrongs while glaring injustices pass without comment. The task of changing public opinion is enormous.

When we attend international meetings, we realize the difficulty of making any real contact between men. They speak different languages; the same words, the same gestures, have a different meaning according to where one comes from; one problem will be of paramount importance to some, and of no interest at all to others. This is not due to ill-will, but simply to the limitations of the human mind. Each one is walled up in his habits of mind and action. He does not even think of trying to understand the other; he thinks only of asserting and imposing on others what to him is important and necessary. All history, all conflicts between nations, bear this out. Yet today it is essential that these peoples should be brought to live and work together. It is imperative. The future of the human race depends on it; civilization can only continue to progress if this is achieved; and if civilization ceases to progress it will collapse; for progress is essential to life, and, if progress ceases, decay sets in. What a problem this is!

If there were only a psychological problem it would be bad enough, but there is also the moral problem!

Man is not only not very intelligent; he is not very virtuous either.

He is selfish. He thinks only of himself. If anyone speaks to him of matters apart from his own interests, he does not listen.

It is true that many men are capable of a good action when their emotions are aroused. There are many examples of this in times of catastrophe; but their generosity lasts only as long as their emotion endures. There again, those who consistently think of others are few. They exist, and they are a credit to the human race; but there are not many of them.

The majority of men are proud. They think of themselves as the centre of the world. When the ancient Greeks made Delphi the centre of the earth, they were expressing a belief which can be found in all peoples in some form or another. For the Chinese, China was the ideal empire. To return to those whom we were discussing before, for the inhabitant of Little Rock what happens at Little Rock is the only thing in the world of any importance, and for the Parisian the important thing is the gossip of the Boulevard. How are we to make an integrated world with men who each think of themselves as the centre?

However, as I reread what I have just written, I feel a certain annoyance, because I am a Belgian, and I have spoken ill of all the world except my own countrymen. Am I also guilty of the universal failing? It would only serve to confirm my theory.

There is no need to emphasize further the moral aspect of the question. I shall return to it when I deal with the attitude of the Christian. Suffice to say, in conclusion, that individualism shows a lack of human development which is not mirrored in the statistics of the United Nations.

According to the usual classifications, under-developed peoples are defined by their material characteristics such as illiteracy, under-nourishment, scantiness of resources and high mortality rate. But would it not be more exact to say that the under-developed man is he who does not concern himself with the world as a whole? This is a definition of a state of mind.

According to this definition, the inhabitants of Little Rock, of whom much has already been said, are under-developed, and so are the majority of Americans. The same applies to Parisians, and to the English, who still think that the secret of power and civilization lies in the isolation of the British Commonwealth. Looking at the matter from this angle I cannot see that any nation could at the moment be considered "developed". The question of development lies in the hands of men, not of nations; it is in the hands of those who are working to achieve the psychological and moral unity of the human race. And a nation will be developed only in so far as it is made up of a large number of men who have international integration at heart, and only in so far as these men are able to carry the mass of their fellow countrymen along with them.

According to this definition the pope, whom we shall quote on this subject, would be a very highly "developed" man. I do not know if he had a refrigerator, or if he watched television, but, in the sense that we have just described, many of those who do have a refrigerator and who do watch television, are under-developed.

This brings us to Christianity, and it is with Christianity that we shall now concern ourselves.

CHAPTER II

UNIVERSAL CHRISTIANITY AND INTERNATIONAL INTEGRATION

Should we say universal Christianity or Christian brother-hood? We are held up at every point by arguments over names. And yet, all this is so well known, has been said so often before, that one wonders if it is worthwhile saying it again. Universal Christianity is a universal brotherhood, and the idea of brotherhood is fraught with both equality and love.

Jesus said to his apostles, before he ascended into heaven: "Go into the whole world, and preach the Gospel to all nations." Christianity is for all men, regardless of frontiers, and it knows no distinctions, either natural or social. St Paul, reacting against the national pride of the Jews, cried out that, among Christians, there was "neither Jew nor Greek, neither bondman nor free, neither male nor female", but that "you are all one in Christ" (Gal. 3. 28). These texts are widely known; my readers have often come across them. Need we go over them again? No, but we should perhaps go beyond the declarations of principle, and the abstract declarations, in order to face up to the concrete facts and ask ourselves how these principles can and should be applied. Since the situation is new, no doubt it calls for new applications. We cannot put new wine into old bottles.

Moreover, general principles are of no use unless they are applied. However, the application differs according to the circumstances.

This has nothing to do with the "situational morality", which is so much discussed these days. Situational morality is a morality which claims that there are no stable moral principles and that each situation calls for different principles. Now stable principles must be accepted; there is a permanent element in human activity; but a principle must be applied differently to meet different circumstances. To apply a principle in the same way to different circumstances is to apply a different principle. To treat a weight of one hundred pounds in the same way as a weight of one thousand pounds is contrary to the law of gravity. If there is a law, the same for all weights, we must know the law. One cannot apply the law of gravity to a particular weight unless one knows the law.

The same is true of universal Christianity. We must apply it to specific facts. Many Christians leave it in the world of theory and react to facts according to other influences. There is a task confronting us today, the task of facing facts. The following pages will show that this is neither so simple, nor so easy, as we sometimes imagine.

THE OLD TESTAMENT

We must go back to the Old Testament if we are to understand universal Christianity.

In general, the only fact we notice about the Jews is their national exclusiveness; and it is true that this dominates the feelings of the Israelites in their dealings with other nations. But this nationalism is in accordance with the doctrinal whole, in which universality also has its place: for Yahweh, the God of Israel, is the Sovereign Lord, the Master of heaven and earth.

He is therefore the God of all men, although he is the God of Israel; all men must recognize him, adore him, submit to him; here we see the beginnings of a universal religion.

However, at that time, this religion was particularist. As men had been unfaithful, and had deserted the true God, this religion was reserved for Israel; it was, so to speak, imposed on Israel; Israel did not discover it, it was imposed on her; and it led Israel along the path it chose. The whole of the Old Testament is simply a history of this leading. Through Israel God remained present in the world; his influence on Israel made it impossible for her to deny or to abandon him.

The Israelites were very aware of this primacy; they were God's people and were contemptuous of all other peoples. This is the dominant feature of their attitude towards the rest of humanity, the "Gentiles". But side by side with this attitude, which is the central element of the Old Testament, which is, so to speak, its main object, for the real object of the Old Testament is to record the vicissitudes of the alliance between Yahweh and his people, side by side with this runs, throughout the book, the more or less casual incidents, and the prophetic texts, which proclaim that God is not indifferent to the Gentiles and that he considers all humanity as his own.

At the beginning of the Old Testament, in the story of Abraham, we read, for example, of Abraham's meeting with Melchisedech. Melchisedech was a mysterious person, King of Salem and at the same time "a priest of the Most High God". He blessed Abraham, who offered him a tithe of the spoils he had collected. Abraham treated him as a superior, and Melchisedech offered a sacrifice of bread and wine, which also seems rather mysterious, because there is no similar offering to be encountered elsewhere.

The figure of Melchisedech has haunted many imaginations; he is spoken of in the psalms; the Epistle to the Hebrews refers to him also. In the highest sense of the word he is *the* priest. Later on the Christian priest says in the Mass: "A sacrifice which ... Melchisedech offered to you." Now the interesting point is that Melchisedech was not of the race of Abraham.

Later on, when Moses led the Jews into the land of Chanaan, the King of Moab, alarmed at the Jewish invasion, sent for the prophet Balaam, who was in Mesopotamia. Balaam was a pagan; he had no connection with the people of God. Yet he is referred to as a man to whom God spoke. None of the prophets of Israel who appear in the rest of the holy Scriptures was more directly inspired by God, or more directly under the divine influence. As with Melchisedech, the Bible recounts this quite simply, without noting any discordance with the normal course of events.

It was exactly the same when the Queen of Sheba visited Solomon; there was no question of contempt for the Gentiles, of whom the queen was one. And the coming of the Magi to the Infant Jesus, at the beginning of the New Testament, but before the new Law had been proclaimed, is of the same character. The Magi were pagans like Balaam —they were priests of the Persian cult—but they were wise men and men of God.

At the time of the independence of Israel, Eliseus raised the son of the Sunamitess from the dead, he cured Naaman, the Syrian, and his activities extended far beyond the bounds of Israel. He was known and venerated in the neighbouring countries, and did not refuse to exercise his powers of prophecy in Syria. He did not seem to think of limiting his activities to the Jewish people. The story of Janos is even more extraordinary, for Yahweh himself, by direct intervention, sent him to Nineve. Yahweh, as he appears in the Old Testament, is not therefore a national God who was only concerned with his own people and who made a rigid distinction between his own people and all others. Although the examples I have taken are incidental and clash somewhat with the general tenor of the Old Testament, and although the Bible is sparing of explanations—here as elsewhere, the Bible tells a story and explains little—yet all these facts show that Yahweh was the Sovereign Lord of all, and although he had chosen the Jews as his special people, he still remained the universal God.

To these facts we must add texts. In the psalms as well as in the prophets mention is made time and again of the messianic kingdom which will extend to the utmost ends of the earth. Yahweh says to his Son: "I will give thee the Gentiles for thy inheritance, and the utmost ends of the earth for thy possession" (Ps. 2. 8). "All the ends of the earth shall remember and shall be converted to the Lord, and all the kindreds of the Gentiles shall adore in his sight" (Ps. 21. 28).

The majority of the prophets echo the same message, especially Isaias: "... He shall bring forth justice to the Gentiles" (Isaias 42. 1), "and the islands shall wait for his law" (*ibid*. 4). "Behold I have given thee to be the light of the Gentiles, that thou mayest be my salvation even to the farthest part of the earth" (*ibid*. 49. 6).

We therefore find this idea nearly everywhere; but we must not exaggerate its importance. These texts represent only a small portion of the Old Testament, and the prophets were reacting against the general attitude of the people. Today we eagerly pinpoint these incidents and prophecies, because what has since occurred has shown that they were portents of the future; but at that time they were swallowed up in a mass of events with which they hardly agreed, and the prophecies of the universal reign of the Messiah could at that time be interpreted as announcing universal domination by Israel.

THE OUTLOOK OF THE NEW TESTAMENT

In estimating the significance of the New Testament in the question which concerns us here, it is less important to quote actual texts, which could perhaps be merely incidental, than to analyse the attitude of Jesus to the situations of the time.

The Jews, conquered and humiliated in the political sense, had intensified their national pride. Having lost their independence they concentrated with even greater pride on their vocation as God's people, and consoled themselves for their present abasement with dreams of future domination nourished on their religious tradition. The indifference which Jesus showed to this attitude, the way in which he stood aloof from national conflicts, his refusal to take part in human, social, professional and even racial distinctions, must have deeply shocked his compatriots. The Jews avoided all contact with the occupying forces; Jesus took no heed of this. However, he made his approach to his own people; he began with them. Although he cured the centurion's servant, although he stopped to talk with the Samaritan woman, these are but minor incidents. Generally speaking, he was surrounded only by Israelites; yet his attitude as well as his words showed a universal outlook.

Above all his attitude was negatively clear. He was completely indifferent to political and social structures. He said no word to indicate that the idea of the kingdom of God could be identified with political domination by the

Hebrew people, any more than he expressed any opinion on class distinctions or on the division of property. These problems were foreign to him. The mission he had come to accomplish was of quite a different order. One of the dominating features of his preaching was that his kingdom, the kingdom which he had come to establish, was to be a kingdom of souls, and had nothing to do with the kingdoms of earth.

The universality of Jesus must have shocked the Jews; on different occasions he asked them insidious questions about submission to the occupying forces. That was the immediate difficulty which faced them. After the death of Jesus the apostles had some difficulty in freeing themselves from their Jewish exclusiveness. However, on the day of Pentecost, the miracle of the Holy Spirit manifested itself before "devout men out of every nation under heaven" (Acts 2. 5), and Peter, inspired by the Holy Spirit, said to his hearers: "This is what the prophet foretold, and it shall come to pass in the last days (said the Lord), I will pour out my Spirit upon all flesh" (Acts 2. 17).

In the early days of the Church undoubtedly the most significant incident was the baptism of the centurion Cornelius. As a result of a vision, Cornelius went to see Peter, and Peter himself had just had a vision which had made him understand, as he himself says, "that God is no respecter of persons, but in every nation he who fears him and works for justice is acceptable to him" (Acts 10. 34).

However, even after this, St Paul had to deliver a sort of ultimatum so that Gentiles could be admitted into the Church on equal standing with the Jews. Such was the power of tradition, of the apparent evidence which had accumulated in the eyes of the people of God. After that, however, the question was never again in doubt, and the doctors of the Church continued to maintain this ruling, as did the pontifical documents themselves.

I do not think it would serve any purpose to quote here all the numerous texts which can be found in every book on the Church. But if we are to understand what the universality of the Church consists of we must recall a few of them.

When the Church calls herself "Catholic" she means that she is universal. In the words of Isidore of Seville, which have often been quoted since, the Church rightly calls herself Catholic, "because she brings together all men and unites all men in her unity" (*De ecclesiasticis officiis* bk I, chapter I).

Even before that, St Augustine had said: "She teaches the same doctrine in every language; some speak African, others Syrian, others Greek, Hebrew, and many other tongues. There is an immense variety but no scission. . . . Whatever the variety of languages, the Church preaches only one doctrine, the doctrine does not change, only the way it is presented . . ." (*In psalm.* 44, 24).

And Rhabanus Maurus says: "All the nations sing the glory of God in the Church, each in its own way" (*De Universo*, 22, 3).

It will be seen that the primary problem was one of language. It seems that political divisions at that time were of minor importance, and that racial problems did not exist. This was in fact true. The hardening of nationalistic feelings for the State is a recent phenomenon, beginning in Western Europe and spreading throughout the world only under European influence. Ancient China, ancient India, ancient Greece, were made up of a multiplicity of States, but still retained a lively sentiment of national unity. What is meant here by national unity is the feeling of belonging to one people, the feeling of being at home in any part of the world. It was the same with Rome, where the division of the Empire into West and East in no way destroyed the moral unity of the Empire. This state of affairs persisted in the Middle Ages. The Spaniards created several king-doms, while remaining fully aware that they were Spaniards, and the Italians formed themselves into many different States, but still retained the feeling of being all Italians. It was in the nineteenth century that the idea of necessarily being identified with a specific State or nation became widespread.

In the same way, the idea of the superiority of the white race took on in the nineteenth century an autocratic nature which it did not previously possess. When the Romans spoke of the Libyans, who are coloured, they did not refer to them as an inferior race; nor, as far as Shakespeare was concerned, was Othello or "the Moor of Venice" a less important person because of his race.

This tradition is maintained in the Church. Even in our time, when the sovereign pontiffs intervene in the question, they speak largely of customs and liturgical language. Thus when Benedict XV instituted the Congregation of Eastern Churches, in 1917, he said "that this act demonstrates that the Church of Jesus Christ is neither Latin, nor Greek, nor Slav, but Catholic".

Christ came to call all men to salvation; the Church continues his mission "seeking only to lead the whole human race to the knowledge of Jesus Christ and to lead it to glory through observance of the evangelical law" (*Instruction of the Congregation of Propaganda to all Missionary Superiors*, December 8th, 1939). In more rous-ing terms, Pius XII said, in his Address *Vivamente gradito* of June 24th, 1944: "Missionary work aims to carry the reign of the risen Redeemer ... to all parts of the world, even to the last cottage and the last man on earth. ..."

CHRISTIAN BROTHERHOOD

Christian universality is a religious universality. We are far from the idea of the aeroplane, although missionaries do travel by air, and the aeroplane has become indispensable to the election of popes, as it enables the cardinals of all nations to meet in conclave at Rome. But we are not so far removed from the moral and psychological conditions of international integration.

However, before considering this question, we can begin by setting out the conditions of universal Christianity which is the basis of brotherhood.

Let us return to the classic text of St Paul: there is among us "neither Jew nor Greek, neither slave nor free-man, neither man nor woman". This is the idea of universality, to be neither Jew nor Greek. In actual fact St Paul speaks only of these two peoples, because he was speaking to them at the time, but he means in effect that there is no difference of nationality among us. At the same period Philip, meeting the eunuch who belonged to the court of the Queen of Ethiopia, and who was therefore coloured, had no hesitation in baptizing him. The apostles did not dream of confining their preaching to the Roman world. It is thought that they penetrated as far as India; at any rate, Christianity rapidly gained ground in Persia.

But in the text of St Paul, "neither Jew nor Greek" is followed by "neither slave nor free man" and "neither man nor woman", which is to say that among Christians all natural differences disappear, "for you are all one in Christ Jesus".

Unity in Christ overcomes all differences between men. When St Paul says: "there are among us neither men nor women", the statement is daring; because if there is any natural difference at all it is surely that. It is as apparent in Christianity as it is elsewhere. Jesus called only men as his apostles, and in the Catholic Church, both in St Paul's time and later, there was no such assimilation of men and women as can be seen in some sects, which leads them to entrust the same functions to both men and women regard-

less of sex. However St Paul does not retract what at first
sight may appear to be an overstatement.

He is so convinced that life in Christ completely dominates nature that the strongest terms seem to him to be
the best. It is true that nature subsists, but it is transformed, and life in Christ brings to the surface a new
element, the importance of which is so far beyond the rest
that all natural differences fade into the background.

The universality expressed in the formula "neither Jew
nor Greek" is therefore only an application of a more
general principle, which is also expressed by "neither slave
nor free man" and "neither man nor woman". The fundamental idea is that of brotherhood, all sons of the same
Father, all one in Christ.

The idea of brotherhood, as I have said, is fraught with
the idea of equality. Brothers share the same blood; and
there is a similarity which is more deeply rooted in the
personality than the differences brought about by life. It is
an equality of a different order from fortune or function,
but it is more profound than these.

At the same time, brotherhood is fraught with the idea
of affection. There is a solidarity among those of the same
blood which is not just the product of circumstances, but
which is founded on a biological reality; one feels something for one's brother. To speak of brotherhood evokes a
sentiment which is dissociated from one's natural inclina-
tions, whereas friendship and even love are based on
elective affinities. Brotherhood, therefore, establishes between brothers a permanent and profound unity. The
Christian brotherhood, founded in God, is a common
filiation to God and a community in the divine life, and is,
in the mind of Christ and the apostles, a far closer brotherhood than any other.

In Christian brotherhood, the unity of blood which
characterizes human brotherhood is replaced by unity in

the life of Christ, and the life of Christ transforms the disciple in a way that the human fact of sharing in the blood of his ancestors can never do.

As the call of Christ is extended to all humanity, so all humanity is called upon to unify itself in him. The Christian vocation is universal in essence and in all directions: it is the rule of unification in all senses among classes, races, nations and sexes. We could also add among ages, to which St Paul does not refer. When a man of sixty—and this man may be the pope—kneels before the statue of Tarcisius, a fifteen-year-old boy whom the older man venerates because he died for Christ, he demonstrates that Christian unity knows no difference in ages, and secs only the life of Christ in the soul, the homage rendered to Christ.

When a Christian world, that is, Christianity, was created in the Middle Ages, the preoccupation with unity was widespread. In the political sphere thinkers elaborated a theory of a Christian republic, and it was in the sixteenth century, in Spain especially, at the time when monarchs began to show national exclusiveness with new rigidity, that the doctrine of a Christian republic, a community of Christian peoples, reached maturity. It was made up of Christians, of Christian people. It is in the brotherhood of Christ that the community of peoples will be created.

THE DOCTRINE AND THE FACT OF THE INCARNATION

All that has been said above must be viewed in the light of the Incarnation, and the Incarnation is above all "God with us", God inserting himself into humanity in order to transfigure it in himself, but doing so without substantially changing the conditions of life. Thus, in the same way that Christ was fully man, and submitted to human laws, growing and acting in accordance with the ways of men, so much so that at first there was nothing to show that he was God, so the disciple keeps intact his human character, even while being transformed by grace. We have just seen that the distinction between men and women subsists, although St Paul has said that there are "neither men nor women" among Christians. In the same way Christianity does not abolish slavery, although St Paul has said that there are no longer either masters or slaves among Christians. Yet again, there are still Jews and Greeks, although St Paul has said that they no longer exist.

All this seems extremely paradoxical, and surely Christianity seems to be reduced to mere verbiage if, after the trenchant words of the Apostle, the same state of affairs exists as before. But, for St Paul, life in Christ is a reality which sweeps away all else, and this reality, which is in his mind, must be transposed into practical life. It is not a statement of a reality already in operation, but a reality destined to be applied.

The fact still remains that the natural conditions of human life remain what they are; life in Christ is on another level, it is the life of the soul, which transforms our spiritual outlook, which leads us to appreciate the worth of other things, which transforms the hierarchy of values, and which exercises through that an influence on all human undertakings, and in this way all things are renewed, although man continues to live according to the laws of nature.

This explains, on the one hand, the enthusiasm of the apostles who proclaimed, under the inspiration of grace, a new springtime of the world: "He who lives in Christ is a new creature; the old things are passed away and behold all things are made new" (2 Cor. 5. 17). But at the same time, everything remains as before; Christianity does not act directly either on political or social structures, or on material life, what today we call technology. The Roman Empire remained, and later on it was succeeded by other empires; Christianity did not advocate a reform of property rights; it did not demand the abolition of social classes; it confined itself to preaching charity, confident that this would act in the nature of a leaven.

Christians are brothers one to another; the master and the slave are brothers; this transforms their relationship; the juridical nature of their relationship is of minor importance if they truly conduct themselves as brothers; the Church does not act directly on institutions, but on hearts. When hearts are in the right place, men will transform the institutions without the Church having to intervene.

It is therefore true that, in the Church of Christ, all men are brothers. There are no longer whites, yellows, blacks or browns. They are all one in Christ. Yet they keep the colour of their skin; they keep their own language, their own human traditions; it is impossible to speak without speaking a language; languages differ from country to country, but there is nothing to say that one language is superior to another, nor that one nation should renounce its own language and adopt that of another. Differences between men arise because of their limitations, and limitations imply plurality. In a limited being there can be no absolute perfection, but many possible perfections, each corresponding to the type of being; each nation develops one aspect of human perfection, or can develop it, but, on the Christian level, all this is founded in the brotherhood which springs from the fact that together we all live in Christ, we take our life from Christ, we live in the spirit of Christ, and everything which is not of this spirit fades into the background.

Unity does not therefore prevent the Church from respecting human individuality. This is shown in the pontifical texts which speak of languages and the liturgy. The Church even respects the diversity of nations. When she spread beyond the bounds of the Roman Empire she busied herself with the conversion of souls, and respected the divisions of kingdoms, principalities and republics. If, as sometimes happened in certain places and at certain times, there arose a tendency to identify the Church with certain forms of civilization, there was always a reaction which affirmed that the Church of Christ is above all that is human. Her task is to imbue all humanity with Christianity, that is, with the spirit of Christ, with divine love.

"I will draw all men to me," said the Master. The mission of the Church is to bring the law of Christ and his life to all humanity, so that all the different ways of life in all classes of human beings, in all the civilizations of the world, should express, each in its own fashion, the charity of Christ.

It is this, among other things, which expresses the idea of Catholicism. Though all men are brothers, they still remain different; though St Paul says that, among Christians, there are neither Jews nor Greeks, free men nor slaves, men nor women, a Jew still remains a Jew, with his own natural temperament, his virtues and his failings, a Greek is still a Greek, a slave is still a slave, a man is still a man and a woman is still a woman. United in charity, man and woman will express this charity in different ways. Because of the limitations of human beings, each will devote his attention to different values, and if all the values that men know are to be offered to God in charity, if the kingdom of God is to spread throughout the world, each human being must contribute his share.

The charity of a woman will show itself in a different way from that of a man, that of a child will differ from that of an adult, as will that of a coloured person from that of a white person, and that of a Southerner from that of a

Northerner. The Church will only achieve her full stature when divine praise is offered up in all parts of the earth, by all peoples, all nations, all races, each paying to the Lord, in its own manner, the homage it is capable of showing.

From one point of view, however, the Church was complete on the day when Christ accomplished his work of salvation and sent the apostles out to all nations; but she was complete in the sense that the seed contains the tree and the new-born child contains the adult. The new-born child already possesses in its entirety the soul which will animate it throughout its life. In the same way the soul of the Church, that is, Christ, was completely active from the first. But the body of the Church is made up of men, and the body of the Church grows in proportion to the number of people who adhere to the Kingdom. This growth of the mystical body will only be complete when all the resources of humanity are coordinated into the service of divine love.

It is because Christianity is a religion of incarnation that the Church can only achieve full maturity through the cooperation of all peoples and of all races. In the early days of the Church, the apostles made particular mention of the fact that, through the love of Christ, human differences fused into the unanimity of charity. But today, after so many centuries, and so many different sorts of happenings, we perceive more acutely that unanimity in charity does not prevent differences of emphasis, and that individual characteristics must remain distinct even while fusing into unity.

Mgr Journet did not hesitate to write that the Catholic unity of the Church will remain in a state of "becoming" as long as there is on earth a single human creature who does not belong to her, or belongs to her only imperfectly and this, of course, not in relation to her fundamental and constituent structure, but to the dynamic fulfilment of her mission (*The Church and the Word Incarnate*). This fulfilment is the fruit of the Incarnation.

UNIVERSALITY IN THE CHURCH

All our remarks so far have dealt with universality of the Church and in the Church. When St Paul says that there are among us neither Jews nor Greeks, he means, among Christians; and the Church has always maintained this attitude. But the problem which faces us today of international integration is quite different, for it concerns not the Church alone; it concerns humanity, leaving the Church out of account; it is not a question of conquering the world for Christ, but of organizing the world such as it is; and such as it is, it is not Christian, or, at the most, only partially so. But in the human or natural situation which it has reached, it needs to be unified. It needs to be unified simply for the purposes of human development. The question which faces us here is not therefore to decide whether Christians should work for the conversion of all men; the need for that was evident long ago and nothing has since changed; it is to decide whether universal organization of the human race is possible and necessary. The question facing Christians in this regard is therefore to decide what attitude they should take in the matter.

The world today faces a new situation, and the problem set by the international integration of the world is a new problem. It is very different from traditional Christian universality, and for this reason it causes a certain amount of uneasiness in many Christian circles. We must therefore carefully examine it, first so that we may become fully aware of the problem, and secondly so that we may understand in what way it corresponds to the tradition of universality in the Church and in what way it differs.

This leads us to reflect on Christian brotherhood. This can be divided into two stages; first there is the brotherhood between Christians, then there is the brotherhood between Christians and the whole of humanity.

When St Paul says: "Among us there are neither Jews nor Greeks", he is speaking of the Christian community, and it is implied that this distinction exists among non-Christians and separates them. More exactly, this saying means that among Christians the distinction between Jews and Greeks is submerged in charity, while this is not so with non-Christians. Generally speaking, we can see that all the texts on the catholicity of the Church, on the duty of the Church to bring all men together, envisage the unification of the human race through and in the Church. This unification is concerned only with the aspects of unity which are achieved in the Church, that is, unity in the Christian faith and in Christian life; it is not concerned with those aspects of unity which are foreign to the mission proper to the Church, for example, the political unification of the world.

With regard to this sphere, the Church accepts the human organization such as it is. If it forms a State, the Church does not intervene in the question of the political value of this State, but simply seeks to obtain the means of furthering its work within that particular political formation.

Christians therefore form among themselves a human brotherhood, and the Church desires to unite the whole human race in this brotherhood. However, at the same time, all men are our brothers, including non-Christians, but these latter are our brothers in a different way.

If we are to understand these distinctions we must refer back to God and bring in a little theology. I apologize to my readers, who no doubt expect something rather different from this book, but there is no other way of elucidating this question without referring back to the Creator.

For God is our Creator as well as our Saviour. As our Creator he is as the origin of all, Master of heaven and earth, and he is also our Father. It is true that Christ revealed the divine paternity to us, but he did not create it. God was our Father, our Father in heaven, from all eternity. Without doubt men would never have fully realized this fact by themselves, and it was necessary for Christ to centre his message on the declaration of the divine paternity, so that it could be given its proper place in the thought of men. Again, even the emphasis laid on it by our Saviour has not succeeded in making men understand. Even many of those who call themselves and believe themselves to be Christians do not see God as their Father, and try to hide themselves from his wrath. . . . But that is another story.

At any rate, Christ revealed to us that God is our Father and that God is Love. He always has been; he did not become so when Christ declared it; he has always loved men; he always has desired their salvation; the new message which Christ added is the way in which God has willed to save us, and Christ is the instrument, the "mediator" according to the traditional phrase, of this way. He is the instrument, the manifestation and the proof.

Nevertheless, before the coming of Christ, the divine love existed. Christ expresses this divine love, he did not create it; and this divine love embraces all men. Christ came to save all men; he called all men to live in and through the divine love. The disciples of Christ partake of his love, and therefore partake of his love for men.

All men are children of God in so far as they are all his creatures. They are therefore brothers. We know that all men are our brothers. Perhaps there are some who do not know it. But we know it. We therefore approach them in a spirit of brotherhood.

However, among Christians there is a special community

and a special brotherhood, into which we desire to bring all others. Baptism makes us children of God; it is a divine adoption. However, all men are, in a manner of speaking, children of God, in so far as they are his creatures, because God is the Father, and this paternity is at the very basis of his relationship with the world. The creative act is the first and fundamental manifestation of this paternity. But we desire that all these brothers scattered throughout the world should become our brothers to a closer degree, so to speak, by being introduced into the Christian family through the divine sonship bestowed by baptism.

There are therefore two degrees in brotherhood, and the mission of the Church is to unify the human race in Christian brotherhood, in which all is at the service of the brotherhood of the children of God.

This leads to a two-way movement; on the one hand there is a sort of exclusiveness, which leads the Christian to concern himself primarily with his brothers in Christ, and to reserve his expressions of charity to them—such as alms to the Christian poor, mutual aid within the Christian community—in short, which leads Christians to close in on themselves in order to form a community of brothers. "Look how they love one another!" was often said of the early Christians: not "Look how they spread their kindness to all", but, "Look how they love one another". They form a community within which charity reigns—but it reigns within the community. Today one sometimes hears of the "Christian ghetto"; it is a fundamental tendency.

The other movement tends to bring all men into this community of brothers. This is manifested through the missionary movement, the incessant propaganda of the Church aimed at gaining souls for Christ. Wherever she is able to contact souls the Church sends missionaries; it is a constant preoccupation of hers. But the primary aim of charity towards non-Christians is to convert them to Christianity.

The reason for this is very clear. The primary blessing for any man is to be a Christian, that is, a disciple of Christ, a partaker in the divine grace. With regard to those who are not Christians, the primary charity is to convert them, for the gift of faith, together with the baptism which follows, is the essential good. The work of the Church, the work of Christians, is to lead all men to Christ.

This is the constitution of the Christian community, whose driving force is directed towards the development of faith and charity in the Church. If kindness is shown to non-Christians, if schools, orphanages and hospitals are established among non-Christians, it is in order to bring them to the faith. The missions perform works of temporal charity, acts of mercy whose aim is to show the benefits of Christianity. We pray for the Church, and for Christians; if we pray for pagans, it is for their conversion; when the faith is persecuted in a country, we pray for the victims of the persecution, for our brother Christians in that country, not for the persecutors. All this is logical; those united in the Church are in agreement about the faith, and they feel that to help non-Christians, without the ultimate reason for this help being to bring them to the faith, implies an indifference to their real welfare which amounts almost to abandonment. For if it is true that Christ is the Saviour, anything which does not lead to him is of minor importance.

Now the question of the international integration of the world is a very different matter. It concerns the creation of a human order embracing the whole of humanity, although the majority of men are not Christians, and do not want Christianity; and we must decide whether we should help to establish this order without first trying to bring men to Christianity, and even without considering whether the establishment of this order will ever bring men to the faith.

If we succeed in establishing a valid order in the community of men which is not based on Christian values, if we succeed in developing a spirit of mutual help outside Christianity, it is possible that men will conclude that Christianity is not essential to the development of humanity. Would it not be better to concentrate our efforts on the development of the Church of God, regardless of the children of the shadows floundering in their wretchedness?

From yet another point of view, the problem of universality set by the international integration of the human race is in itself very different from universal Christianity.

Universal Christianity is, so to say, a desire, an achievement at which the Church is aiming, a spirit. The Church had a universal spirit from the first, because our Saviour assigned to her the task of converting the whole earth; she was universal by vocation; but she was not universal in fact. In fact, the early Church was a seed which developed progressively, and which gradually spread throughout the world; but men continue to live without the Church, in so far as they are not converted. The Church is preoccupied with universality; she continually maintains that she was instituted for all men, that she welcomes all peoples and all races on the same standing. Today she has given an outstanding example of this universality by the formation of native clergy. But here it is a question of a unique and homogeneous society, which began as a small group and spread gradually, maintaining its homegeneity and its unity.

On the contrary, the problem of the international unification of the human race is that of the unification of numerous independent societies, which have developed independently from, and often antagonistically to, each other, each absorbed in its own affairs, and it is the development of material civilization which enables them to be unified, and which at the same time renders this unification essential if civilization is to continue to progress. On the one hand we have a problem which must be rapidly resolved, or we are faced with collapse, and which must be resolved as a whole, through an agreement between peoples. On the other hand we are faced not, as in the case of the Church, with a progressively developing society, but with a collection of societies which must somehow be federated. There is a colossal difference.

Can Christianity contribute something to this undertaking of international integration, and ought Christians as such to take part in it? It is not surprising that many Christians are uneasy. From childhood they have continually been told of Catholic works, of Catholic charity, of the support of Christians everywhere and of the propagation of the faith; they have been urged to pray for persecuted Christians, against persecutors, and when urged to pray for non-Christian peoples, it is to ask for their conversion. Must we now break away from this well-balanced arrangement in order to help unbelievers without considering their conversion? It is in truth an entirely new problem and we are not prepared for it.

CHAPTER III

THE TEACHING OF PIUS XII

THE FIRST CONFERENCES

In 1898, the Tsar of Russia took the initiative in calling a conference to discuss the subject of peace, with a view to persuading the European States to disarm. Leo XIII immediately supported this in two addresses at the beginning of 1899. The first Peace Conference was then convened at The Hague. The Queen of Holland wrote to the pope, at the request of the Tsar, and Leo XIII replied indicating his desire to place all the influence of the Church at the service of peace, and taking the opportunity to point out the international character of the Church: "The Church's action in promoting the general welfare of humanity rises above the particular interests which the various chiefs of State have at heart, and, better than anyone, she knows how to bring into harmony so many peoples of such varying types."

At that time the question was one of peace and not of a general organization for cooperation. Moreover, it only concerned Christian nations. It was of them that Leo XIII was speaking; this was only natural, as he was aware that no other question was under discussion, and in fact, no other question existed at that time. However, the Tsar of Russia was Orthodox, the Queen of Holland was a Protestant; neither country had diplomatic relations with the Holy See: Leo XIII did not refer to this. He showed his readiness to collaborate with them to the full and spoke of the Tsar only in the most glowing terms.

During the Boer War in 1900, Leo XIII again addressed the Sacred College on March 2nd, asking them to pray to the Lord for those who were suffering in the war: "They are all his sons and our brothers who are carrying on this terrible conflict. . . ." Now the belligerents on both sides were Protestants. The pope was not at all concerned with that; somewhere there are men suffering: we must go to them.

Already we see the attitude which was to be that of all the popes. Pius X had few occasions to intervene in the matter, but the reign of Benedict XV (1914–22) was completely dominated by the First World War. He continually intervened, primarily with the immediate aim of preaching peace, but always awaiting an opportunity to put forward constructive proposals. On August 1st, 1917, he sent a letter *To the Belligerent Peoples and to their Leaders* which is a sort of charter for essential universality, and which put forward ideas which henceforth were to dominate the century.

First of all, the fundamental point must be that the moral force of right shall be substituted for the material force of arms; thence must follow a just agreement of all for the simultaneous and reciprocal diminution of armaments, in accordance with rules and guarantees to be established hereafter, in a measure sufficient and necessary for the maintenance of public order in each State; next, as a substitute for armies, the institution of arbitration, with its high peacemaking function, subject to regulations to be agreed on and sanctions to be determined against the State which should refuse either to submit international questions to arbitration or to accept its decision. Once the supremacy of right is thus established, let all obstacles to the free intercourse of peoples

be swept aside, in assuring, by means of rules, to be fixed in
the same way, the true liberty of and common rights over
the sea, which on the one hand would eliminate numerous
causes of conflict, and, on the other, would open to all new
sources of prosperity and progress.

At that time rumours of peace were beginning to circu-
late, and Benedict XV wanted to support the efforts of
those who sought to put an end to the terrible conflict.
Those who advocated a fight to the finish received this
pontifical move with bad grace; but, with the passing of
time, it appears today as a momentous date in universal
history. Benedict XV referred to it after the war. In 1920
he made a general examination of the situation in the
Encyclical *Pacem*.

The League of Nations was born; the pope alluded to
it when speaking of the necessity for a general coming
together of all peoples:

> The natural relationships of dependence and mutual ser-
> vice which unite the nations have become closer than ever
> as a result of a keener sense of civilization and the astonish-
> ingly increased facility of communications.... It would be
> really desirable that all States, having put away their mutual
> distrust, should join together in a single society or, better, in
> a family of peoples.

But Benedict XV was convinced that the undertaking
would be in vain if it were not established in the spirit of
Jesus Christ. When he addressed the former belligerents
he begged them

> in the name of our Lord Jesus Christ to bury for ever all
> their differences and mutual wrongs and to re-establish be-
> tween them the sacred bond of Christian charity which
> knows neither enemy nor stranger, and then we earnestly
> call on all nations to conclude among themselves a real
> peace in a spirit of Christian good will and to make a pact
> of union that justice will make lasting.

Benedict XV made no distinction between those countries which were Catholic and those which were Protestant
or Orthodox, and there were even pagan countries in the
League of Nations. He spoke of "re-establishing between
them the sacred bond of Christian charity" as if this bond
had previously existed. But this bond had never existed
for Turkey, China or Japan. Benedict XV, however, was
perfectly definite that he considered that, outside Christ,
it was useless to seek a common ground of agreement
among nations. But if unity between nations can only
be sought for in a spirit of Christianity, should not the
nations first be converted to Christianity, and should not
Christians first seek to convert their brothers? We find
ourselves faced with the question with which we ended the
previous chapter.

Although the idea of a universal society crops up in
the passages just quoted, the pope still remained dominated
by the viewpoint that the fate of the world depended on the
European nations. These nations were traditionally Christian; some of them had cut themselves off from Rome, but
Rome had never accepted this separation as final, and
continued to address the Christian world as the Mother of
the Churches.

After this the reign of Pius XI extended over the dis-
tressing inter-war period, when the world painfully sought
to find a balance. The pope did not cease to urge peace
among men, and to give tokens of his sympathy to all who
contributed to the development of international order; but
it remained for Pius XII to define the doctrine.

THE UNION OF THE HUMAN RACE UNDER THE NATURAL LAW

Before he was elected pope on March 2nd, 1939, Pius XII
had been papal nuncio in Berlin, and secretary of state. As

such he had collaborated intimately with Pius XI during the latter's last years. In 1937 the Encyclical *Mit brennender Sorge*, addressed to the bishops of Germany, on the errors of national-socialism, illustrated the importance of the natural law in social life. The question was of major importance at that time, with the German situation as it was. We may be sure that the former papal nuncio to Berlin was no stranger to the Encyclical.

> Such is the rush of present-day life [said the pope] that it severs from the divine foundation of revelation, not only morality, but also the theoretical and practical rights. We are especially referring to what is called the natural law, written by the Creator's hand on the tablet of the heart (cf. Rom. 2. 14), and which reason, not blinded by sin or passion, can easily read. It is in the light of the commands of this natural law, that all positive law, whoever be the lawgiver, can be gauged in its moral content, and hence, in the authority it wields over conscience. Human laws in flagrant contradiction with the natural law are vitiated with a taint which no force, no power, can mend.

From his very first Encyclical, *Summi Pontificatus*, of October 20th, 1939, Pius XII followed up these ideas and extended them to include the whole world:

> Before all else, it is certain that the radical and ultimate cause of the evils which we deplore in modern society is the denial and rejection of a universal norm of morality as well for individual and social life as for international relations: we mean the disregard, so common nowadays, and the forgetfulness of the natural law itself, which has its foundation in God, almighty Creator and Father of all, supreme and absolute Lawgiver, all-wise and just Judge of human actions. When God is hated, every basis of morality is undermined; the voice of conscience is stilled, or at any rate grows very faint, that voice which teaches even to the illiterate and uncivilized tribes what is good and what is

bad, what lawful, what forbidden, and makes men feel themselves responsible for their actions to a supreme Judge.

The denial of the fundamentals of morality has its origin, in Europe, in the abandonment of that Christian teaching of which the chair of Peter is the repository and exponent.

This passage deserves to be read with attention, because it gives a complete summing up of the situation. Social life is based on the natural law, and this is founded in God. It is traditional to teach in the Church that when belief in God is abandoned the natural law and natural morality collapse; but Pius XII shows here a moderation which evinces great care to avoid all exaggeration: "the voice of conscience is stilled, or, at any rate, grows very faint", and at the same time he shows that, to his mind, the natural law is not necessarily linked with Christianity, since he reminds us that the notion of natural law is found even in primitive peoples.

On the other hand, in Europe the moral and the natural laws had been closely integrated into Christianity. This had given Europe a moral cohesion which had led it "to such a degree of civil progress that it could teach other peoples and other continents".

Consequently, in abandoning Christianity, Europe was abandoning all that had given her her dignity and grandeur. As far as Europe is concerned, it cannot be too strongly emphasized that her fate is linked with that of Christianity. Europe had been Christian: each time the pope returned to this subject it was to repeat that Europe would never be herself again unless she returned to Christ and the Church. However, the problem of human relationships today is not limited to Europe. On the international plane we meet peoples who have never been Christian. With them, we must return to the natural law which "teaches, even to the illiterate and uncivilized tribes, what is good and what is bad, what lawful and what forbidden".

Since then, Pius XII constantly made use of every

occasion to review every aspect of the international situation. It would be difficult to count the number of times he intervened, in day-to-day happenings, first during the war to reduce suffering, to appease hatred, to prepare for reconciliation, to recall the principles of a stable and just peace. Then, after the war, he intervened in all the painful events which followed year after year. Like those of his predecessors, the interventions of Pius XII usually corresponded to the prevailing circumstances. He was not merely a professor content to pass on abstract teaching; he was the leader of the Church, the father of all the faithful; he had to guide them in the delicate questions of the moment which troubled their consciences. But every so often he returned to the idea that morality and the natural law must guide the conduct of nations. Sometimes the words "natural law" were not used, and Pius XII confined himself to recalling the virtues required for political order. Sometimes he judged it necessary to recall that the question was one of natural law, which is imposed on us all.

In the Christmas message of 1941, when the war was at its height, Pius XII spoke of the foundations which must be laid for a new order:

> This new organization which all peoples desire to see realized after the trials and the destruction of this war ought to be founded on the immovable, unshakable rock of the moral law as it is made clear by the Creator himself by means of the natural order, and written by him in the heart of man in ineffaceable characters: it is that moral law whose observance must be inculcated and cherished by public opinion in all nations and all States with such unanimity of opinion and force that no one can dare to throw doubt on it or weaken its obligation.

As soon as hostilities ceased in Europe, he broadcast a radio message (May 9th, 1945) on the conditions necessary for a return to order:

Merely to confine ourselves to Europe, we are confronted with enormous problems and difficulties which must be overcome if a way to true peace is to be made ready, for it is only peace of this kind that will be lasting. And it can only develop in a climate of assured justice and entire honesty together with mutual trust, understanding and good will. The war has produced everywhere discord, distrust and hatred. If the world desires to find peace again falsehood and rancour must disappear and in their place truth and charity must reign as sovereigns.

We find ourselves here on the plane of natural morality. Pius XII brings to bear his whole influence in order that men, all men, whoever they may be, should unite in the work of reconstruction. It has sometimes been said that the Holy See is the highest moral authority in the world. We see here this authority being fully utilized, guiding, as it were, the whole world in the path of the natural law.

As far back as 1939, in his first Encyclical, *Summi Pontificatus*, Pius XII said:

We are hoping for a new order of things, which will govern the life of peoples and adjust their mutual relations, when these unnatural conflicts, these cruel butcheries, have died down at last. This new order must not be founded on the shifting standards of right and wrong, treacherous as quicksands, which have been arbitrarily devised to suit public and private interest. It must stand firmly based on the immovable rock of natural law and divine revelation. From these the giver of laws must derive his principle of balance, his sense of duty, his gift of prudence; if they are forgotten, the line which divides a legitimate from an unjust use of power is all too easily overstepped. It is only if he acts thus, that the awards he makes will have any intrinsic stability, such as the august sanctions of religion can give; if he acts otherwise, it will be found that they have been dictated by self-interest and greed.

The years go by but the teaching remains the same; Pius XII continually returned to the subject and he defined it in increasing detail. A complete and systematic statement of his ideas is laid out in the important discourse which he gave on October 13th, 1955: "The first postulate of all action for peace is recognition of the existence of a natural law common to all men and all peoples."

The international problem is today no longer a European problem. It was European in the nineteenth century. Since the beginning of the twentieth century nations of other continents have progressively appeared on the scene, and among them there are the peoples of Asia who have no Christian tradition. After the Second World War the international problem, and more precisely the problem of cooperation between men, became radically worldwide; the whole of Asia was emancipated and Africa began to seek its independence. A man of our time cannot limit his interests to Europe. Pius XII was well aware of this. However, with half the human race a stranger to Christian traditions, agreement could only be reached on the natural level. The pope appealed to the human race to unite on the level at which it can unite.

The Church has always taught that the natural order cannot be separated from the supernatural, nor the natural law from the positive law established by Christ. By virtue of the mission she has received to conserve and transmit the deposit of divine teaching, it is up to her to define the natural truths as well as the supernatural truths, when they concern the moral order. As a result of this, natural morality has gained from the teaching of the Church a precision, a coherence and a vigour which cannot be found elsewhere. However, this morality remains a natural morality; it corresponds to the needs of human nature, it corresponds to the highest aspirations of man; these aspirations are often confused, but they are nevertheless permanent. Sometimes, under the sway of certain fallacious theories, attempts have been made to turn men away from

this morality, but after a certain time nature reasserts itself
and men return to the fundamental ideas which accord with
their nature.

The Catholic Church plays a decisive rôle in this sphere,
and renders a service the importance of which is more
clearly seen in our time than ever before. The world is in
a turmoil of contradictory and passionate theories. As the
guardian of morality and the natural law, the Church continually recalls to mind the fundamental bases of this
natural order, and she alone gives this teaching; but Catholics are not the only ones capable of hearing. In this way
she extends her rôle as a sort of spiritual director of the
human race.

THE RÔLE OF CATHOLICS IN INTERNATIONAL LIFE

What must the Church, the Catholics, do? Pius XII
did not neglect to tell them:

A heavy responsibility weighs on Catholics: above all they
must realize that they are called to overcome international
narrow-mindedness and seek true brotherly understanding
between nations.... From their childhood they have been
taught to look on all men without distinction of race,
nationality and colour as the creatures and the image of
God, redeemed by Christ and called to an eternal destiny,
to pray for them and to love them. No other human group
offers such favourable conditions from all points of view
for international understanding (*Allocution* to those taking
part in the *Congress for International Understanding among
Peoples*, July 16th, 1952).

As far back as the Christmas message of 1941, which
we have already quoted, Pius XII when speaking of the
reconstruction of the world after the war, said:

Not only this or that party, this or that country, but all
peoples, the whole of humanity, with a perfect sincerity of

will and energy must work together at it. It is a universal
undertaking for the common good which requires the collaboration of Christendom for the religious and moral
aspects of the new construction.

These words clearly show the way. However, Pius XII
was aware that many would feel lost in the novelty of the
situation. In the preceding chapter I outlined the reasons
for this uneasiness, which in some has turned into resistance. For this reason the pope returned to the problem;
once more he acted as father of the faithful; he was not a
professor content to lecture from the rostrum; he was a
father who urges, in season and out of season, as St Paul
says.

The question of international order is undoubtedly the
first and most important social question in the world
today. Pius XII was continually thinking of it; he mentioned it on every occasion, neglecting no details, not only
in relation to the needs of this order but also the part
that Christians have to play. We can consider a few of the
most significant passages:

The faithfulness of the Catholic Christian to the divine
heritage of truth bequeathed by Christ to the teaching
authority of the Church in no way requires him, as many
people think, to offer a mistrustful reserve or cold indifference in face of the serious and urgent duties of the
present time. On the contrary, the spirit and the example of
our Lord who came to seek and to save what was lost, the
precept of love, and, in general, the social implications to
be found in the Gospel, the history of the Church which
shows how she has always remained the strongest and most
constant support of all the forces for good and for peace,
the teaching and exhortations of the Roman pontiffs,
especially during recent decades, about the behaviour of
Christians towards society and State—all this shows clearly
the obligation incumbent on the believer to concern himself, in accordance with his state of life and the means at

his disposal, with courage and unselfishness, with those questions that a sorely-tried and upset world must solve in the sphere of social justice no less than in the international order of law and peace. The convinced Christian cannot confine himself to a convenient and selfish isolationism when he is witness of the needs and wretched state of his brothers, when requests for help from the economically weak reach him, when he is fully aware of the aspirations of the working classes for more normal and juster living conditions, when he has full knowledge of the abuses of an economic theory which places him above social obligations . . . The Catholic doctrine on the State and civil society has always been founded on the principle that by divine will peoples form a whole, a community with purpose and duties in common. Even at a time when the proclamation of this principle and its practical consequences raised very sharp reactions, the Church refused her consent to the erroneous conception of an absolutely autonomous sovereignty which should be exempt from social obligations. The Catholic Christian, convinced that every man is his neighbour and that all peoples are members, with equal rights, of the family of nations, eagerly associates himself with those generous efforts . . . which tend to make States emerge from the narrowness of an egocentric mentality (*Christmas Message*, 1948).

The above text is again one which should be read attentively. In one page he gives a complete statement. He speaks openly of Catholics who practise a so-called supernatural "isolationism" with regard to questions concerning the world on the natural level, and, beginning with the Saviour himself, he recalls the constancy of the Christian tradition of pursuing all human good in all its various aspects.

Should Christians therefore throw themselves unreservedly into neutral international organizations and never unite among themselves? The Christmas message of 1955 discusses this question. Undoubtedly, it says, Christians should unite in Christian organizations with a view to acting in concert in the world; but, even in these institutions, "they have no other purpose than that service desired by God for the good of the world".

If they were not held back by the respect due to the person of the sovereign pontiff, some "devotees" would have rebelled at this, for the pope teaches in plain terms that we must not seek direct conversion in this sphere. We must work without thinking of the ultimate welfare of the human race. This work must be organized on the level of the natural order. This is absolutely obvious, providing the questions are viewed without prejudice and the solutions which result are arrived at with a view to answering the needs of mankind. But, on the international plane, we must be content with that.

The idea that Christians should band together and consecrate themselves solely to supernatural values, and the idea that to enter into the temporal interests of humanity without an ulterior motive shows a lack of supernatural feeling, seemed to be strongly held in Catholic circles, for the pope again attacked this question with increasing energy. He desired Catholics to take upon themselves the problems of the world; he did not want them to be supernaturally cut off from the world; he was inflexible on this point. In the Christmas message of 1957 he took up the theme again, insisting even more vigorously than before that

> cooperation in the order of the world required of the Christian by God must avoid that spiritual approach which would forbid him all intervention in external matters and which, adopted as an attitude by Catholics, occasioned serious harm to the cause of Christ and of the divine Creator of the world.

Pius XII was therefore well aware that he was preaching a new attitude of mind; the idea of the Christian shutting himself up in a Christian circle is the traditional attitude, but "it occasioned serious harm to the cause of Christ". The conditions of our time show the necessity for a very different outlook. The Christian must be supple; he must be able to adapt himself. The rôle of the supreme pontiff is to show the way.

Are then the two plans of action, the one on the temporal level where we must work with unbelievers on the basis of the natural law, the other on the supernatural level where we must work to convert the world, completely unrelated, and must we put one of them on one side while we work on the other? The uneasiness of many people arises from the fact that they do not see how to reconcile the two positions. But Pius XII never lost sight of the unity of Christian work. He said in his Christmas message of 1945:

> The Church is supranational because she includes in the same love all nations and all peoples, but this supra-nationality does not place her as if suspended in a remote and inaccessible region above the nations; on the contrary, just as Christ was among men, the Church, in whom he continues to live, is also among peoples; just as Christ took on a genuine human nature, the Church takes into herself the fullness of all that is authentically human, making of it a source of supernatural strength in whatever place and under whatever form she finds it.

The natural order is a preparation for the work of conversion. If the world understands that it can find in the Church the instrument of all progress, how can it help turning to her?

CHAPTER IV

THOSE WHO FORM THE CHURCH

The last chapter was a doctrinal outline, defining what is the duty of Christians. But will they do their duty? To call oneself a Christian is not sufficient to make life adapt itself automatically to Christian teaching in all its aspects. Pius XII's teaching on the international situation is an extremely appropriate example of the way in which the intervention of the teacher applies unchangeable Christian principles to changing realities. But will Christians play the part in the world to which he called them?

If we are to determine what can be expected of the Church we must take into account the reality of the Church. Now this reality is something apart from her teaching. The reason for teaching is for it to impregnate life. Christ did not come merely to teach a doctrine in order to have the intellectual satisfaction of inculcating us with the truth; Christ is the Saviour; he came to reveal to us the joy of salvation and the object of doctrine is to show us the way. The final objective is therefore that men should save themselves, and to do that they must first establish Christian order upon earth—Christian order both in their individual lives and in their lives together.

Now this cannot be achieved by the pope alone, or even by the pope and the bishops. The Church is made up of the whole body of Catholics. To be a Catholic doubtless implies that one is linked to the pope and the bishops, but they are only the leaders of the Church. It is true that this hierarchy gives a form to the Church, and thanks to this hierarchy we know where the Church is and what it is to be a member of the Church, but it is none the less true that the Church is formed by the whole mass of Christians, of whom the pope and the bishops form a part, for the pope is a member of the Church as well as being its leader. To be the leader of the Church one must first be a member.

Consequently, the hierarchy teaches and shows the way, but the action of the Church is accomplished by the body of Christians. It could be said that the Church is like an army in battle. The general cannot fight the battle on his own, nor can he win on his own. He gives the orders, decides the movements, leads the troops, but if the soldiers do not follow him he can do nothing by himself. When the battle starts it is the troops who fight. In the same way, the pope shows Catholics the path to follow; but are they following? Besides, how many Catholics even hear of the pontifical instructions? How obedient are they? The question is not only to know whether they should obey, but do they obey? In short, for us who are now face to face with the question, which of us know what Christians should do, and secondly, do we know to what extent Christians can be expected to follow the pontifical instructions?

It is no longer a question of doctrine, nor of morality, but of fact. This is quite another viewpoint, and the majority of those who study the question are perhaps too quick to believe that it is sufficient to lay down principles, and that after that there is no problem. But the problem facing us now is more or less to ask ourselves to what extent those who are called "Catholics" really are Catholics, or rather, what we mean by "Catholic". We shall never come down to earth until we have carefully examined this question.

THE CATHOLIC MASSES

According to statistics there should be about 475 million Catholics in the world, and some people are disillusioned when they read this figure. "How is it," they say, "that after nearly two thousand years, the Church of Christ includes only 20 per cent of humanity, when Christ came to call all men to salvation! Does this not make a mockery of the Redemption, and is this failure compatible with the doctrine according to which the Church is the instrument of universal salvation?"

The statistics mean different things to different people. Others, more optimistic, observe that Catholic Christianity is not the only form of Christianity but only the perfect form; that, if we add the Protestants and Orthodox Christians there are about a thousand million men who believe in Christ, which makes 40 per cent of the human race, and that if we add those who adore a single God, without being Christians, we arrive at more than half the human race, and perhaps two-thirds recognize the sovereign Lord of the universe.

In actual fact these discussions are futile. It is useless to waste time on them. We who know that the Church is the messenger of God and the Bride of Christ, established to accomplish his work on earth, have simply to ask ourselves to what extent and in what way she can accomplish this mission, and what resources she has at her disposal.

But, in accepting that Catholics number only 20 per cent of the human race, many people are astonished and aggrieved that they do not have more influence on the world, and that the Church, through them, has not more influence. To explain this we must analyse what these Catholics are.

When we say that there are 475 million Catholics in the world we are referring only to the number of baptisms. It is a canonical definition, that of canon law, which is the law of the Church. Baptism is the introduction into the Church; all those who are baptized are therefore Catholics, whether or not they practise, believe, or live up to its morality. These are merely "statistical" Catholics, that is, Catholics who are counted in the statistics, but statistics take no account of the influence of religion on their ideas and on their life.

The majority of the most notorious anti-clericals, who laboured to dechristianize France, were Catholics in this sense: they were usually baptized; the majority had even received religious instruction and had made their first communion; many were married in the Church. But they then spent their whole lives working against the Church.

I have often read articles about the countries of Latin America where the Church has been persecuted; and it is noticeable that 95 to 98 per cent of the population are Catholic; we pity these poor Catholics harried by anti-clericals. But what is never mentioned in these articles is the fact that the persecutors form part of the 95 to 98 per cent Catholic population in these countries, and that many of those, who are accounted Catholic in the statistics, undoubtedly share their opinions!

The statistical number of Christians therefore gives no indication of the influence that the Church can wield. This number only takes account of the number of baptized Christians, including those who show no other act of loyalty to the faith as well as the most ardent Catholics who consecrate their whole life to God, to Christ and to the Church. The pope, the bishops, the clergy, the monks and nuns form a part of this number, in the same way as the baptized persecutors.

After dealing with the statistical Christians, we come to the practising Christians. A few years ago, inquiries were made into religious life almost everywhere, and fairly similar situations were found in all the countries with a Catholic tradition, that is where statistical Christians form the bulk of the population, and baptism is a part of the national tradition, without necessarily being related either to faith or to life.

In urban centres, it was found that practising Catholics generally formed 15 to 30 per cent of the population. In some districts, this dropped to less than 15 per cent. An inquiry in a parish of about 10,000 inhabitants, in a large town in Chile, showed 300 practising Catholics, that is, 3 per cent. . . . Yet Chile is an entirely Catholic country, statistically speaking. The situation in rural districts varies greatly from country to country. There are rural districts where 95 per cent of the population attend Sunday Mass, and others where only 5 per cent attend. We need not make any detailed analyses here; the fact which interests us is to know what the Church can expect from these Catholics.

In the inquiries those who attended Sunday Mass were called "church-goers", or "Easter-duty makers", that is, those who made their Easter duties. A large proportion limit their Christian life to this.

In the mass, these are the "confessional Christians", that is, those who have sufficient faith to confess their sins, and therefore to repent, to a certain extent, while they are going to confession—when I say "to a certain extent", it is because this number includes those who go to confession, for example, to please someone else, maybe their wife or their mother, but who would not go on their own initiative —and who have not sufficient faith to fight against sin. For them, religion is reduced to a religious practice which has little effect on their life. Their religion is mainly "sociological", that is, it depends entirely on their social environment, and is completely impersonal. They do as others do in their environment.

ACTIVE CHRISTIANS

Among the number we have just been speaking of there are a certain number of active Christians, some of them visibly active, in particular those who wear a uniform, like the clergy, the others lost in the masses, and having no outward sign to show their quality. They can be recognized by their works, but those who do not see their works cannot distinguish them from the rest. For example, those who take part in a Catholic Action movement, in the Legion of Mary, in the *Pax Christi* movement, even many who do not take part in any movement, but who pray and are charitable to those around them. Who are these Christians, and how many of them are there?

Who are they? They are Catholics absorbed in their Christian life, those to whom Christianity is important. They could also be called "personal Christians", that is, their attachment to the Church is not just the result of the social environment in which they live, but a personal willingness more or less independent of their environment. These Catholics are therefore interested in the Church, which has for them an intellectual and active character. Intellectually speaking, they want to understand the requirements of their faith; actively speaking, they want to fulfil these requirements.

How many of them are there? It is impossible to say. Many more inquiries into religious sociology would have to be made before any idea of them could be reached. However, it can be said that there is an increasing tendency today to identify the quality of the Catholics with that of the active Christians. A Catholic leader once said to me: "We estimate that there are still ten million Catholics in France." And when I asked him, "What do you mean by Catholics?" he replied: "Those who are prepared to make sacrifices for the Church." These are not statistical Christians, nor confessional Christians.

Active Christians are the only ones who can be directly influenced by the teaching of the Church on particular questions, such as, for example, the attitude of Christians towards the international integration of the world. The statistical Christians are indifferent to the refraction of Christian thought on life, and their opinions are not formed through contact with the Church; confessional Christians identify religion with worship and some rules of personal morality. There are therefore only a limited number of Christians to accomplish the work of the Church and spread the thought of the Church among men, by which I mean, not only among non-Christians, but among statistical Christians and confessional Christians.

Are there one hundred million such Christians in the world? I doubt if there are as many. Moreover, amongst even these, how many can be counted upon?

I knew a woman who was extremely pious and very anxious to serve God, and who had great devotion to St Teresa of the Child Jesus. She bought statues of St Teresa and took them to all the priests in the district asking them to put one in their church. Then she went back to make sure that the statue had been put in a good place. These statues were extremely ugly; what interested her was that they should be large and not too expensive, because she was not very rich.

She spent all her time on this activity and all her available money; she was undoubtedly an active Christian, but it is difficult to see what direct service she was rendering to the cause of the international integration of the human race. Perhaps she was giving an indirect service; we shall return to this later on. At any rate, at first sight it appears that her initiative could have little bearing on the international scheme of things.

This example leads me to another point, which is that Christian faith and life extends over an extremely vast field, a field too vast for one man to take in all on his own. For that reason, active Christians specialize, and their initiative or Christian zeal is concentrated on one aspect of doctrine or life. A professor of dogma may spend his

whole life studying the fundamental problems of Revelation, the Trinity, the Incarnation and the Redemption, but
he may never succeed in having a practical influence on the
international order—which is so practical and so far from
fundamental doctrines. Another may be preoccupied in
studying the liturgy or the holy Scriptures, yet another in
studying family problems. Again, these people are undoubtedly active Christians, but although their personal
thought and action are inspired by Christ, they do not
bear any relation to certain aspects of faith or Christian
action.

How do they form their opinions on other subjects?
They have not reflected on these questions, which are of
secondary interest to them. Their ideas therefore come
from what they have drawn from their environment.

However, environment is not entirely under the influence of Christ; it is subject to other influences. Many
opinions and ideas develop under the domination of all
kinds of circumstances, which lead to a development
foreign to Christianity, and which may even lead, without
anyone realizing it, to a development opposed to Christianity. Some active Christians therefore find themselves,
without being aware of it, with a state of mind which is
not Christian.

If, in the environment in which I am born, I hear from
my infancy, and as an incontestable truth, that my country
is the most civilized of all, the most civilized and the
most Christian, to the extent that Christianity is identified
with the tradition of my country, that the greatest good
which other peoples could enjoy is to assimilate the culture
of my country, and that the best means of christianizing
pagans is to inculcate them, at the same time, with the
national language and spirit of my country and its ways of
life; if I have never heard anything but this, how shall I
not believe it, and how shall I see that it does not conform
to Christian brotherhood and to the principle of the equal

right of all men to develop according to their own character? This is an abstract form of describing the missionary drama of the nineteenth century and the beginning of the twentieth century. The young man who entered a seminary or a noviciate, after having been impregnated throughout his youth with the idea that his country was the chosen land of Christianity, the messenger of Christ to other nations, and having been taught also that the white race was the superior race, that European civilization was the best of all civilizations, and that the future of civilization was identified with the domination of the white race and the form it had given to civilization—this last is moreover a mark of our present time: hitherto it was not considered that the civilization developed by the white race was a *form* of civilization among others; it was thought that it was *the* civilization, and that no other existed—this young man studied philosophy and theology in the purely abstract sense, and then went out as a missionary; but, as far as identification of Christianity with his country was concerned, he kept the ideas formulated by his environment. His teachers, his superiors, were moreover in the same case. Where would they find other ideas? They had heroic courage, unlimited devotion, inexhaustible charity, but all this was saturated with a collective contempt for "inferior" peoples and civilizations. This is of immediate importance to the question which is the subject of this book, for the international organization of the human race requires a spirit of universal brotherhood, which sees the "similarities" in all men, and which approaches in a spirit of welcome, composed of esteem and sympathy, the problems of other peoples.

LIKE A LEAVEN

The kingdom of God is like a leaven in a dough: the missionaries I have just spoken of were full of charity, but

the leaven cannot make the dough rise except in the way
the nature of the dough allows it to rise.

We are speaking here of human works and contacts. If
the missionary does not see the qualities of the people
he is working among, if he himself believes, and that sin-
cerely, that his own people have qualities superior to all
other peoples, his action will deviate from its aim. In the
nineteenth century, and at the beginning of the twentieth
century, when the question of the workers arose, many
Christians reacted in a manner opposed to the requirements
of Christian brotherhood. In particular, a fairly large number of those who were preoccupied with the liturgical
movement, were conservative in their social outlook, giving
their approval to the majority of the abuses of authoritarian
political régimes, to social régimes based on inequality, and
to economic régimes based on injustice. None the less, they
were active Christians; they were preoccupied with Christian values, but their attention was turned to the Christian
values contained in the forms of worship. Where all else
was concerned, they accepted the attitude of their environments. Today the same situation is to be found with regard
to international action, and the pontifical interventions,
which we have quoted above, clearly show that a resistance
of the same kind is being put up by a certain number of
active Catholics.

This explains the pontifical interventions, as well as
showing the efficacy of them. At first sight, it would
seem that it was only necessary for the pope to speak, and
all active Christians at least would follow the path he
indicated. But the very words of the pope show that this
is not so. We find ourselves back again at the law of the
leaven: when the pope addresses the Christian world, his
word also is like the leaven in dough; it acts according
to its own purity and also according to the aptness of the
dough which it penetrates.

The word of the pope is like a leaven. But the leaven only acts on the dough which it can reach. Who is reached by the word of the pope? It does not reach the whole world. Some hear it on the radio; others read summaries or quotations in the papers. But the radio programmes and the newspapers which draw attention to these pontifical interventions—I am speaking of those interventions dealing with the international law—are few. Many of their listeners and readers pay little attention to what is said. Even the text of the pontifical interventions can only be found in publications which have small circulations, and are rarely read except by a small number of specialists.

The reader can find this out for himself by reading these pages: this short book will certainly give to more than one an impression of discovery, because the pontifical texts which have been quoted have never attracted his attention. But again, what sort of circulation will this book have? Perhaps a few thousand copies will be sold in a world of two and a half thousand million inhabitants. Many of those in the foremost ranks of active Christians, concerned with the liturgy, the Bible, the Ecumenical Councils, will not be influenced by it. Many active Christians, moreover, have simple souls, preoccupied by their immediate interests, incapable of raising their eyes to perspectives beyond the horizons of their life; they are busy among the poor and the sick; they spend their time doing good to those around them; but, again, this problem is foreign to them; their opinions on this matter are formed by the ideas which they have adopted from their human environment, and they are completely ignorant of the pontifical interventions; they do not even know if the pope is concerning himself with the question, and they see no relation between the teaching of Christ and U.N.O.

In consequence, we have succeeded in limiting more or less exactly the number of those who can be relied upon

to spread throughout the world the teaching of the popes,
and to bear witness in the world to the way in which the
spirit of Christ is applicable to the present-day problem of
the international integration of the human race. They cannot be numbered in hundreds, nor yet in dozens, of millions.
It is a relatively restricted group, this little flock of whom
our Saviour was speaking, when he said to his disciples:
"Do not be afraid ... my little flock. Your Father has
determined to give you his kingdom" (Luke 12. 32).

MOVEMENTS OF OPINION AND PERSONAL ACTION

To complete our understanding of the way ideas are
spread and how human opinions respond to them we must
also distinguish between several strata of minds.

All collective action depends upon a diffused attitude
of mind, spread throughout an environment and more or
less impregnating it, and corresponding to its acceptance,
which is often, simply, acceptance in one environment of
something which is not accepted in another environment.
For example, the idea of the superiority of the white race
and the identification of civilization with the civilization of
the white race was generally accepted in the nineteenth
century and up to 1914. No one thought of querying it; the
coloured peoples themselves in general admitted it. It was
equally accepted by Christians, and in particular, by Catholics, that there would be no true development except in
Christendom, that this was the privilege of the white race,
that there could be no authentic human development in
other races except by becoming Christians, and that in order
to do so they must stand in line behind the whites.

In our days, on the contrary, the conviction has spread
that civilization is not necessarily linked with the destiny
of the white race, that Christianity is not linked with it

either, that civilization can be developed outside Christianity, but that Christianity can and should exercise its influence upon it like leaven in dough, that, as Pius XII said, "no other human group offers such favourable conditions for international understanding because Catholics, from their childhood, have learned to look on all men as the creatures and image of God". Moreover, if humanity cannot attain complete fulfilment except in Christ, none the less, taking it as it is, Christians must first show what the love of Christ is, by the part they take in the development of universal brotherhood among men, and to this extent the attitude of Christians must be modified, and this modification will have very profound repercussions in very different spheres.

Opinions will change spontaneously in proportion to the extent that these ideas are spread, an attitude of welcome will develop towards foreigners and men of other races, the obstacle of national pride will melt away, and this modification of opinion and attitude will not be limited to active Christians; doubtless it will be begun by a certain number of active Christians, first of all by the pope, then by others, like the author of this book who echoes him, and by movements of various forms which will bring together those active Christians interested in the matter, for example, the *Pax Christi* movement, which unites Christians interested in spreading the Christian conception of life in the international order.

In the proportion to which this attitude is spread, more and more Christians will be drawn towards this action, still more Christians will sympathize with the developments of international action, will take part in different international movements, and, little by little, the whole body of the Church will modify its trend.

It is to this that Mgr Dell'Acqua was referring in the letter of April 8th, 1957, when he said:

All Christians, even those whose profession or apostolate is exercised in their usual daily life, are invited to open their eyes to these vaster perspectives, and to make their contribution to the establishment of greater justice and charity. All must be made aware of what Catholics working on the international level are achieving, what they themselves can do to support their action, what the Church expects of her sons in a world in which relationships are being brought closer together, without however, always becoming more human.

In this way this action works on opinion, which prepares the way for an authentic Christian conception of relationships between peoples. The specialists play a personal rôle. First there are those who sit in international assemblies and organizations; then there are the technicians who give their services to under-developed countries. Both must work in a spirit of Christianity, and they will be formed in this way to the extent in which their environment is saturated with this spirit. In an environment saturated with the spirit of international collaboration, vocations to international service will be developed. Yet, even today, ardent Catholic environments too frequently remain apathetic when one speaks of world problems or of the problems of collaboration on a worldwide scale. Now if a technician enters an international organization or accepts a mission of service to an under-developed country, without understanding the part his activity is to play in developing combined human relations, if he accepts the post merely to earn his living, or to further his career, he will fail to bring to his activity something which is essential, from the Christian point of view, even though his skill may be perfect.

When the *Pax Christi* movement undertakes, for example, a campaign on the subject "My brother, the foreigner", it forms opinion, it encourages initiative, and indirectly prepares Christians who tomorrow will collaborate with all their human brothers to form a more united humanity.

HOW GRACE WORKS

The catechism defines grace as a supernatural gift of God, which enables the soul to partake in the divine life and prepares man for eternal life. This could be called an ontological definition; it explains what grace consists of, but says nothing of its effect on earth.

Grace is therefore a spiritual reality, resulting from the active presence of God in the soul, and conferring a divine character on the acts of man. Grace has the effect that man thinks and wills in accordance with God. This homogeneity of man with God is intensified in proportion to the extent in which grace penetrates man.

Since grace is the presence and action of God in man, it is also the presence and action of God in the world through every man who is in a state of grace. In proportion to the number of men in a state of grace, and in proportion to the intensity with which grace works in them, it acts through them, that is, God acts through them in the world. The action of God in the world is essentially the action of men in a state of grace. This brings us back to the law of the Incarnation.

The effect of grace is to guide our spirit and our will to conform with the divine spirit. Undoubtedly, through the law of the Incarnation, this action of God is brought to bear on a human spirit which is subject to other influences, but, to the extent to which man permits the divine action to act on him, this action eliminates the opposition and develops a spirit conforming to the divine will. Grace is both a dissolvent and a stimulant; it dissolves what is contrary to the divine spirit, it reinforces what is conformed to it, it guides the spirit towards divine preferences.

This action of grace is strongly noticeable in a small number who are impregnated with it. For example, in moments of crisis, when over-excited passions develop into hatreds, which are often fed under honourable pretexts, such as patriotism, some Christians who live their Christian life intensely find as if by instinct the delicate balance between love of country and love of one's enemies, and are able to take part in the combat without allowing themselves to be imbued with hatred. But grace also exercises a collective action. For men are interdependent; they act one upon the other, ideas are spread and are linked to effects which pass from one to another. The development of grace, which is identified with the development of charity, induces a repugnance for all which is contrary to charity, and guides the spirit towards that which encourages charity. "Charity is patient, charity is kind", says St Paul (1 Cor. 13. 4–7). If, in my human environment, there reigns contempt for anything that is not of my class or of my race, charity will react against it.

One man on his own is generally incapable of reacting against ideas deeply rooted in his environment, and forming the traditions of the environment. In aristocratic times, there were saints belonging to the upper class, accepting the unjust privileges of that class, but making use of those privileges in order to practise towards those belonging to an inferior milieu a goodness which did not exclude the fact that they were aware of their superiority. But, when the movement of ideas conforming to the Christian outlook spread, the good Christians were more accessible to it, and in proportion to the extent that some of them worked to spread those ideas, they spread more easily when those whom they reached were the more saturated with grace, when the level of grace was higher in the environment.

When I speak of the high level of grace in the environment, I mean, since grace exists only in souls, that the level of grace is high in a great number of people. To the extent that it is high and to the extent that it exists in a great number of people, so to that extent all trends conforming to grace will spread; all trends contrary to grace will be thwarted.

As regards the question with which we are dealing here, the fundamental Christian trend is towards the universal brotherhood of men ("my brother, the foreigner") a sentiment of equality and similarity—all sons of the same Father—benevolence, absence of a critical attitude of mind etc., all the things which were lacking in the nineteenth century. All this is now developing, and is developing in conjunction with a general development in personal Christian life. Now the life of God in us through grace is eminently personal. The divine life of the "sociological" Christian, who believes and who practises because he is made to do so by his environment, is extremely problematical.

In this sense, even the good soul I mentioned above, who used her apostolic zeal in putting up statues to St Teresa of the Child Jesus wherever she could, is indirectly working for the cause of universal brotherhood, in the sense that devotion to St Teresa is a holy devotion, which authentically develops the Christian spirit. Perhaps she could have used her zeal in a more judicious fashion; perhaps she would have done if she had been better led; but taking the facts as they are, to the extent that any such activity raises the general level of grace, so those trends which conform to the spirit of God find easier access to souls.

To take an illustration used by Pius XII, Jesus compared grace to light. The higher the light is placed in the candlestick the more it shines; the purer the light the more it illuminates its surroundings. The light of Christ dissipates the shadows of error; the love of Christ dissolves pride and selfishness. But, if the light of Christ is to shine we must be more than just "statistical" Christians.

If the light of Christ is to spread throughout the world, it is essential not that there should be a greater number of baptized people, or even a greater number of practising Christians, but that the level of grace should rise higher in the human race.

CHAPTER V

THE QUESTION OF WAR

We might just as well say, the question of peace, for peace is the contrary of war; if war is to be avoided peace must be established; and, for peace to be established, war must be avoided. It could also be said: war or peace. It all comes back to the same thing. If I prefer to talk of war, it is because it is war which troubles everyone's mind.

Since the end of the Second World War, terror has weighed heavily upon the world, due to the invention of nuclear armaments which threaten nations with total destruction. Several of those who have read the preceding pages will undoubtedy have felt a certain annoyance at the calm way I have dealt with international cooperation, when the threat of war seems to cast all that into the shade. What is the good of talking about international cooperation when everything could be annihilated by the atomic bomb? "Total armament" is a tragic beginning for any cooperation. Let us first avoid war and then see what happens.

This is collective fear. Now fear is practically the most degrading of all human emotions. Fear makes a man lose his human character, because the man who is afraid flees from danger with no other thought but to flee, and he is unable to reflect. Reflection implies calm, mastery over oneself. In panics many deaths are brought about solely by the fact that everyone fled at once, blocking up the exits and preventing everyone escaping because no one thought of anything but escape.

When faced with the dangers of war, the main thing is to keep our heads, and when the war becomes more menacing the need for keeping our heads increases. We are therefore going to try to reflect calmly upon this.

WAR IS A CONSEQUENCE

The first point is that war, like peace, is not a cause, but a consequence. War is the result of men not agreeing, but agreement implies moral conditions. The first condition for peace is agreement.

Peace will never be more than a truce until there is an agreement of hearts. As early as 1920, just after the peace treaties of the First World War were signed, Benedict XV wrote in the Encyclical *Pacem*:

> Although almost everywhere, in some way or another, war has been stopped and treaties of peace signed, the seeds of former disagreements have not been destroyed.... All peace is unstable, all treaties are ineffectual, despite long and laborious negotiations by their authors and the sacred character of the signatures placed on them, so long as a reconciliation inspired by mutual charity does not quell hatred.

Two years later, Pius XI took up the same idea in his first Encyclical, *Ubi arcano Dei*:

> Peace was indeed signed in solemn conclave between the belligerents of the late war. This peace, however, was only written into treaties. It was not received into the hearts of men.... The task, urgent above all others, is the pacification of minds. Little can be expected of an artificial, external peace, regulating and governing mutual relationships between men, like rules of behaviour; what is required is a peace which penetrates and calms minds, opens hearts and unifies them in brotherly love.

Pius XI continued to repeat this throughout his whole reign. As for Pius XII, as soon as the Second World War broke out, he began to speak of peace and the conditions of a just peace.

War is a consequence. It follows distrust between nations and the various forms of national pride and egoism which lead each nation to consider itself virtuous and to believe that its rights are threatened by the covetousness of others. Peace implies trust, but trust is impossible without a minimum of esteem; if I think my neighbour is a robber, what can I do but defend myself against him?

But is he a robber? This is a question of fact which cannot be viewed objectively unless one is able to observe objectively and to reflect. It is easier not to reflect, to act simply upon emotion, "a Communist will stab you in the back", or, "once a Nazi always a Nazi".

Peace implies trust. But we can only have trust if we achieve a state of organized collaboration, for without that each one is left to himself and must take every precaution on his own. Yet no collaboration can be organized except in an atmosphere of trust. It is a vicious circle that we have been pursuing for forty years; but, if we want to find a way out, we must begin with trust.

Since the end of the First World War, the urgent need for international cooperation has been recognized. This resulted in the League of Nations; but the League of Nations failed, because people's hearts were not ready for it. The teaching of the popes aimed at making Christians artisans of the union of hearts.

There must be moral action: international organization will be possible only in so far as men as a whole understand the need for it. In so far as there is an efficacious international organization, to wage war will become difficult to the extent of becoming impossible. While there is no efficacious international organization, the chance of war will lie in the hands of those who believe they have the power to wage it.

Peace is therefore based on an attitude of mind, on a sentiment. This sentiment grows, but its growth is slow compared to the speed at which circumstances change. It is because of this that, at least since the end of the First World War, all serious thinkers and all who have studied the question state that there must be a definite end to war, and yet no such achievement has been reached.

During the inter-war period, a powerful study movement grew up among legal writers, which ended in a general condemnation of the "war procedure", that is, a condemnation of the attitude that war was the normal means, the final resort, for the protection of rights. It was therefore concluded that only defensive war was legitimate, and there followed an attempt to define what a defensive war was. It is obvious that if the whole world agreed to renounce offensive war, there would never be a defensive war.

This is the legal attitude: the Church bases her attitude on morality. She does not have to concern herself with positive right; positive right is a technical term; if the whole world agrees to avoid war, the necessary legal formula will be found. The rôle of Christians as such is to bring about understanding. This does not mean that those Christians who are in a position to intervene in international questions should not put forward positive solutions; it is desirable to have as many Christian lawyers as possible; their Christian spirit will lead them to seek the means for cooperation.

Facts, as we have said, have altered more quickly than attitudes of mind. It is obvious that agreement is essential to a stable peace. As early as 1894, Leo XIII, protesting against the armaments race in a letter to the princes and nations of the world, spoke of the "coming together of nations, a thing so desirable in our time for the prevention of the horrors of war". But all evolution in modern times has also included the sense of the absolute independence of States. These States will admit no authority above them, and when conflict arises and it has not been possible to resolve it by peaceful means, recourse to violence has been the last resort. Before the First World War, the right of States was never questioned: attempts were limited to persuading States, by various means, to accept arbitration or to renounce certain methods of warfare. In this way war itself became a legal state; the law of war was often spoken of, and during the First World War the Germans were accused by many of having violated a certain number of the laws of war.

Nations have been imbued for centuries with the idea of the sovereignty of the State, and these opinions have evolved slowly, whereas, in our century, the conditions of social life have been transformed much more quickly. In Chapter I, were noted the obstacles preventing international integration of action. Nations, on the whole, are made up of men who do not live internationally, or who live in this way without being aware of it, as one does when one eats food which comes from the other end of the world. International integration, in all its forms, is therefore the work of a small number; but international organization implies at the very least that men as a whole should accept it as a matter of course.

I know some old Bretons who to this day speak of England as an hereditary enemy. Yet France has not fought against England since 1815. However, their opinions were formed by listening to tales of the seventeenth and eighteenth centuries. In their eyes Jean Bart was almost one of their contemporaries.

On the other hand, the Germans have invaded France three

times, in 1870, in 1914 and in 1940. Every Frenchman over the age of twenty can remember the invasion. It is not surprising that the majority of them find it hard to believe that war is no longer possible between France and Germany. "Since they attacked us yesterday," they say, "why should they not do the same tomorrow?" This reasoning, which is so simple and so apparently common-sense, seems much more conclusive than the reasons which militate against them, and which are complicated and require long explanations.

But, if we wish to arrive at the truth, we must, here again, be prepared to view the situation in its reality.

WAR AND WARS

First there must be calm. Systematic optimism and systematic pessimism are equally dangerous; both are infectious and are based on the character of the subject and not on the reality of the facts. But, as has been said, the more dangerous the situation the more necessary it is to keep one's head and be objective. It is impossible to be objective unless the mind is clear, and the mind cannot be clear unless one's nerves are under control. The surgeon who has to perform a delicate operation needs to be the calmer the more serious the operation. Efficiency and agitation are in absolute opposition to each other.

Now, when we try to consider the question of war in its reality, it must be remembered that war as such does not exist; there are only many different wars. People have been working for nearly forty years to prevent wars. During the inter-war period war was declared "outlawed", yet this spectacular measure has not prevented it. The simple people once again say proudly, with their apparent good sense: "War has always existed; it always will exist."

However, there are a great many things which have

always existed—until they disappeared. Take slavery, for example. It has not, perhaps, entirely disappeared, but it has, at any rate, ceased to be a universal institution, and it is hunted down wherever it still exists. There are also some who want to maintain poverty, on the pretext that there have always been rich and poor people! But there is a varying number of poor people; we cure one cause of poverty, and then another cause.

So it is with war. War in itself is an abstraction; there are many wars, all different from one another. Each war has certain determined conditions; certain forms of war disappear; others appear.

One form of war may disappear; once there were wars between families, between tribes; these wars have disappeared; there have been wars between principalities; finally, in the Western world, war is no longer possible except between States.

However, no form of war becomes impossible all at once; it disappears slowly, as a result of social changes; but the consequences of former situations remain for a long time, and this is yet again a result of the slowness already referred to several times, with which minds become aware of new situations and adapt themselves. Even to this day, examples of this can be seen in certain sectors of society; reference is often made to the Corsican *vendetta*, but, in other countries as well, we find, from time to time, similar phenomena.

On the other hand, war and conflict are not analogous. Even if war became impossible there would still be conflicts; they are two different ideas.

This leads us to another apparently sensible argument, which is often voiced. "You want to suppress war," we are told, "but do you think that men will stop arguing?"

This is true; if the suppression of war could only be

brought about by men agreeing with each other in every matter, there would be no chance of stopping wars. However, not every conflict is a war; war is a conflict which takes a definite form, and this form of conflict can be suppressed without suppressing the conflicts themselves.

For example, competition in business has never been as strong as it is today. Yet the managers of a great store in New York or London would not think of sending their staff to make a machine-gun assault on a rival store and set fire to it. They would perhaps have done so in the Middle Ages. However, the newspapers are full of the stratagems used by financiers, industrialists and business men to destroy each other. The conflicts remain, but recourse to certain methods has been eliminated.

War is essentially recourse to force of arms. Other means of action and pressure exist. After the Second World War a great deal was said about the "cold war", which was understood to mean a systematic state of hostility in which every means of destroying the enemy were used except recourse to arms. The danger of the cold war is that it increases hostility and at the same time renders any collaboration impossible. And if cooperation disappears completely, to be replaced by systematic and constant hostility, the danger of a "hot" war, or war pure and simple, increases day by day. War still remains in the strict sense of recourse to arms.

Is war still possible? This question will make some readers smile, and others perhaps indignant. However, smiles or indignation will undoubtedly betray the feelings of the speaker, but will give no indication of the objective reality.

When we ask: "Is war possible?" it does not mean that we believe that war is going to disappear one fine day from the face of the earth, by a wave of a magic wand,

and that one minute men will be fighting each other on all sides, and the next minute they will be shaking hands with each other. If war disappears, it can only do so by a slow and progressive resorption of each war, not of war as such, since war itself is an abstraction, and there exist only many wars, all different, each having its own characteristics, its own causes, its own incidents, conducted by different men who have different customs and different weapons, each war lasting for a different length of time and fought in different countries. We must take all these elements into account when we ask ourselves, not whether war as such is still possible, but whether such and such a war is possible, and, to begin with, between what countries, and under what conditions.

When the question is put in this way, we must first take into consideration that war today is unthinkable in the greater part of the world. This is indeed a fact.

Looked at from this point of view, I think I can say that war is now impossible between France and Switzerland, or between France and Belgium. However, France is a much more powerful country than the other two. But, being a Belgian myself, I can truthfully say that there is no Belgian who is afraid that French regiments are going to invade Belgium, and no Swiss has such fears either. Does this mean to say that these countries are always in perfect agreement? Not at all; there are conflicts all the time. Even in the last few years, France has been litigating against Switzerland on the subject of free zones; there has been a great deal of talk about it, but no one has thought of going to war.

Between France and England, or between France and Spain, it seems that war is not possible. Although all these countries still maintain their armies, it is not through fear of each other. I am not speaking of Germany, where circumstances are a little different, because there was a war with them less than twenty years ago. If this war does not threaten to break out again it is because something has changed in Germany, something very profound; I have not to study this matter here. I merely wish to show that war seems an hypothesis which does not apply to the whole of Western Europe.

The United States of America has 175 million inhabitants, and Canada has sixteen million. They share a common frontier more than 3,000 miles long, along which there is no fortification. I think I can say that not one American citizen thinks of a military invasion of Canada, and that no Canadian, not one, fears an American military invasion.

I am speaking of military invasion, for Canadians fear an economic invasion; but that is quite another matter. War is a military operation, and no one is thinking of war. Yet the United States could overrun Canada in a very short time. It is obvious that they are the stronger, and no one could come to the aid of Canada sufficiently quickly. Yet war is an hypothesis which does not apply.

Let us take yet another example at the other end of the world. India has more than 300 million inhabitants, and Ceylon has less than ten million. Under English rule Ceylon was part of India. She is now separate, and does not appear to fear an invasion from India, any more than India appears to think of invading her. We could go round the whole world in this way. Nearly everywhere war appears impossible.

THE WAR OF ANNIHILATION

Despite this, terror hovers over the world. It arises from the total armament which, since the atomic bomb, continues to be perfected, and which threatens humanity with a destruction of which no one can estimate the consequences.

Yet even when faced with this weapon, we must keep our heads.

I quoted above the words of Leo XIII, who was faced with the arms race of sixty years ago; they are not very different from what is being said today. The 1914 war ended with experiments in gas warfare, and during the inter-war period it was constantly stated that the next war, if it took place, would be a bacteriological war. When Marshal Pétain became a member of the French Academy, he described the total destruction which would result from such a war, and a special edition of *L'Illustration* analysed in detail the way in which the population of Paris would be annihilated. When the Second World War broke out, everyone was issued with gas masks. This distribution, however, only served to enrich the manufacturers.

However, poison gases existed; they could have been used. Each of the belligerents held the formula. But experience has shown that the most dangerous weapons are not necessarily used. This does not arise from moral scruples, but simply from the fact that there would be no advantage in using them if the other side were able to use them with equal effect.

It is admitted today that there is a possibility of war, not between every country, but between the two most powerful States of the world, the U.S.S.R. and the U.S.A., and Western Europe feels that it may well be implicated in the conflict. This explains the uneasiness which reigns in countries like France and England. Moreover, even countries which do not fear to be implicated in such a war, like the Far East, or South American countries, are more or less apprehensive, for the consequences may be so disastrous that they would affect the whole human race.

What is to be done in these circumstances? First of all, we must not lose our heads.

Next, everything possible must be done to prevent the

war. However, as we have seen, war is a result. It is therefore necessary to bring our efforts to bear on what causes war, not on war itself. Those who spend their time making propaganda for peace are often like gardeners who spray the leaves of a tree so that it will bear good fruit. It is the roots which need spraying; we must attack the roots of war.

If wars are to be prevented, a spirit of international cooperation must be developed, and in the proportion to which this spirit is developed, so institutions will spring up. As cooperation develops, so the risks of war will decrease. But to try to make war impossible between peoples who hate each other is a waste of time.

Moreover, all the weapons which have been perfected in the twentieth century are related to scientific developments. The latest weapons, in particular, are the result of developments in physics, chemistry and mathematics, and the discoveries which serve military purposes can also serve to improve human life. This development cannot be stopped; but it could be prevented from destroying humanity in proportion to the degree to which men are united.

The most effective action against total armament is therefore to develop a spirit of collaboration among nations. However, it must not be forgotten that total armament does not substantially transform war; we have noticed that for more than fifty years people have been speaking in more or less the same terms. The aim remains the same; an international society must be formed, in such a way that all nations can be drawn into a network of mutual aid which will stifle the desire for war.

In proportion to the extent to which attention is given to the cooperation and development of the whole of humanity, so will nuclear science tend towards the achievement of pacific aims.

One danger remains. Each of us must die; the present danger is that we may all die together, or that at least a great number may die at once. To be afraid changes nothing; we must keep a cool head if we are to calculate what can be done to avoid this.

THE MOVEMENT FOR PEACE

As a reaction against the uneasiness let loose by the danger of war, movements for peace have been developed practically all over the world, some organized and some spontaneous, some big and some small. Side by side with the organized movements there is in public opinion a widespread belief that peace must be safeguarded at any price, and that peace is the only thing which matters.

There are two centres in these movements for peace. The first is in Russia, and extends throughout the Communist countries. The movement for peace is organized here with the approval and under the control of the government. Although the whole world does not actively participate in it, it nevertheless exercises considerable pressure on the masses, and the aim of this movement is to proclaim the desire for peace among peoples. The movement starts by assembling the peoples of the Communist countries, then an appeal is made to non-Communist peoples to associate themselves with the movement.

However, this movement does not try to influence in any way the Communist State. It is based on two simple ideas: first, that the capitalist powers are preparing a war of aggression; secondly, that the whole world must be appealed to to prevent it. The Communist State declares that it will defend itself if it is attacked, and does not hide the fact that it is preparing for this. The Communist peoples have *a priori* trust in their governments; they do not allow them to be questioned.

The government of the U.S.S.R., moreover, declares that it possesses nuclear weapons, and that it will use them if war breaks out. It does not in any way consider that this attitude is contradictory to its support of the peace movement. This is explained because, in actual fact, the peace movement simply aims at uniting the peoples of the world in universal action with a view to preventing the capitalist governments from perpetrating the crimes for which they are preparing.

The peace movements in countries with parliamentary freedom are completely different. In these countries it is possible to question governmental policy and to lead campaigns of opinion without the approval of the government. Peace movements, in this part of the world, are started by those who are acutely aware of the threat of war, impressed by the ravages which this war might produce, and disillusioned that their governments do not take effective measures to ward it off. According to them, war must be condemned, and there should be a refusal to prepare for it, condemning defensive war as well as offensive war, saying "No" to war. That is all. If the whole world said "No" to war, there would be no war. These movements are closely linked with the movement of conscientious objectors. In Communist countries no attention is paid to them. The Communist countries are also preparing for war, and we have no means of bringing pressure to bear on them. They never question the matter.

To sum up, the peace movement in Communist countries aims only at disarming capitalist countries; and the peace movements in parliamentary countries aims at the same objective. No peace movement aims at making the Communist countries disarm.

In these movements, peace appears as a value to be directly pursued for itself, and not as a result of international order.

Pius XII spoke a great deal about war and peace. His whole reign was dominated by this question and there is no other question upon which he commented so often. His attitude is the centuries-old attitude of the Church which has simply been adapted to our century.

The Church has always fought against war. In the litanies of the saints we find the phrase: "Deliver us, O Lord, from pestilence, famine and war!" War is a scourge from which we purely and simply ask God to deliver us.

However, it must be remembered that the Church has always admitted that there could be a just, or at least a defensive war, without naming actual cases, which are usually extremely complicated. She judges war to be a scourge, and she has tried to check it and mitigate it. In our times, she has encouraged everything which has tended to eliminate it, since the first Peace Conferences.

Pius XII incessantly repeated that war, especially in the guise in which it appears in our time, is a crime. He who begins a war is therefore a criminal. However, as long as criminals threaten war, as long as there is no security from aggression, nations must be capable of defending themselves.

There are two principles: modern war is a crime unless it is undertaken "under an unconditional need to defend oneself", on the other hand,

> the community of peoples must make allowances for the existence of unscrupulous criminals who do not fear to let loose total war to fulfil their ambitious plans. That is why if other peoples desire to protect their existence and their most precious goods and do not wish to leave free rein to international brigands, it only remains for them to make ready for the day when they will have to defend themselves (*Allocution* to the members of the Sixth International Congress of Penal Law).

On careful reading this text illustrates, on the one hand, the condemnation that the Church has always formulated against war and all forms of violence, but, on the other hand, it shows that it is based also on a judgement of fact. Each one has the right to defend himself against robbers; he who is responsible for others has the duty to defend those who are in his care. Pius XII considered that in the situation in which we find ourselves today, it is not impossible that robbers should still exist in the international order. Consequently, honest men, that is, peace-loving peoples, must be ready to defend themselves.

A little before this, on September 13th, 1952, Pius XII said to members of the *Pax Christi* movement: "No State or group of States can calmly accept political servitude and economic destruction. For the common good of their peoples they must assure their own defence." However, he never separated peace from the organization of international order. "Defence tends to check attack but also to obtain that political and economic measures are honestly and completely adapted to the state of peace."

Agreement between peoples even implies that each one should be ready to defend himself, and that all should defend each other:

> The thought of the Catholic and of the Church is realist. The Church believes in peace and does not weary of reminding responsible statesmen that even the present political and economic complications can be resolved in friendly fashion given the good will of all the interested parties. On the other hand, the Church must take account of those evil powers which have always been at work in history. That is the motive for her distrust of all pacifist propaganda in which the word peace is abused to cloak undiscussed aims (*Allocution* to the members of the *Pax Christi* movement, September 13th, 1952).

This passage needs no commentary to enforce its point. In the face of those who desire peace at any price, without taking account of anything else, the pontifical view appears, in effect, to be profoundly realistic.

Christian desire for peace is practical and realist. It is of an entirely different temper from the simple feeling of humanity which is too often founded on mere impressions and which only hates war because of the harm, atrocities, destruction and dire results it brings in its wake, and not for its injustice (*Christmas Allocution*, 1948).

"The Christian desire for peace is as strong as steel": but, it is practical, and stands apart from extremism. There are a great many extremists in this field, in complete opposition to each other; there are a great many simple minds, impressed by the danger and ready to jump from the frying-pan into the fire. Pius XII was obliged to return to the subject, and to make his point specifically again, since no one wanted to understand. In the Christmas message of 1956, he explained in even greater detail how he judged the actual situation, and how it justified his attitude. Pius XII mentioned facts which should be borne in mind. The Second World War was due in large measure to the fact that Western Europe had lost its combative urge and neglected its military preparations at a time when Hitlerism was arousing in Germany the instincts of a wild beast. From 1933–9, Hitler struck successive blows to test the ground, to see if he could advance with safety, and no one stopped him. When France and England were finally compelled to oppose him with force over Dantzig and Poland, they found themselves unprepared, and we know what followed. Pius XII's view was that this should not happen again; only the thoughtless youngsters who know nothing of history, even of recent history, and who live in a purely emotional atmosphere, could gainsay him.

The multiplication of new weapons increased the growing uneasiness. On all sides, Pius XII was subject to advances on the part of members of peace movements, urging him formally to condemn atomic warfare. He ended by deferring to them, and in an address to doctors, on

October 19th, 1953, after recalling what he had always taught on the subject of war, he added: "What we have just elaborated applies primarily to atomic, biological and chemical warfare. It will be enough for us to have raised the question whether it can become merely necessary for defence against total war carried out by these methods. In this case the answer is to be deduced from the same principles which are decisive today in allowing war in general."

We again encounter the word "today". Pius XII always dealt with the situation of the moment; one day, perhaps, war will no longer be possible, and the Church desires this ardently; she never ceases to do what she can to lead peoples to the agreement which will bring this about; unfortunately, that day has not yet arrived.

The following year, speaking to another congress of doctors, on September 30th, 1954, Pius XII returned to the question of modern, total warfare in greater detail:

> On principle, the question of the lawfulness of atomic, chemical or biological warfare cannot even be raised except in the case in which it is judged to be indispensable in self-defence under the appropriate conditions. Even then, however, every effort must be taken to avoid it by means of international agreements, or to place such clear and narrow limits on its use that its effects are confined to the strict requirements of defence. When, however, the use of this means leads to such an extension of the evil that it entirely exceeds man's control its use must be rejected as immoral, for it would no longer be a question of defence against injustice and of a legitimate safeguard of legitimate possessions, but of annihilation pure and simple of all human life within the sphere of action. And this cannot be allowed on any grounds.

I have quoted this passage in order to give the reader an idea of the shades of meaning in the pontifical attitude.

Pius XII differentiates between several hypotheses, but remains firm on the principle that everyone has the right to defend himself with the same weapons with which he is assailed. The partisans of peace at any price and of unilateral disarmament were evidently disillusioned. Some wanted to twist the pope's views, by interpreting them as an absolute prohibition, applicable in all circumstances; others said: "The pope is in favour of war." Someone even wrote to me: "The pope condemns atomic, biological and chemical weapons; he therefore considers it legitimate for men to kill each other with flamethrowers." I fear that it would be useless to try to make such people understand anything.

THE THREAT OF WAR RECEDES

To suppress war is therefore a false problem. The true problem is to make the threat of war recede and gradually fade away. Or, more exactly, as war does not exist in itself, but only many wars, all different, all linked to concrete causes, the problem is to render such and such a war impossible, then another war, and so on, one after the other, till they all become impossible.

Now the events of the last years seem to indicate that in principle the only possible war is that between the two dominating powers, the U.S.A. and the U.S.S.R. Apart from that, there seems no dangerous threat except in the Near East, in the territory between Egypt and Turkey. On several occasions, military operations have been started there since 1950, but the intervention of the United Nations has shown itself capable of arresting their development. Again, at the moment there are United Nations observers in several parts of the world. Although the United Nations is not officially endowed with a police force, and although it is rent internally with conflicts between parliamentary states and popular democracies, yet the power of a police force is in fact developing and already appears effective.

On the other hand, the development of international relations has had, as one of its effects, that of making various countries seek mutual sympathies outside any military alliance, which leads to the fact that the importance of states is becoming increasingly independent of their military power. When, in 1955, a conference of Asian and African States was held in Bandung, the whole world press heralded it as an extremely important event. Twenty-six Asian and three African countries were represented there, numbering more than half the human race. For the first time an international conference which excluded Europeans and Americans was held. However, what was undoubtedly the most remarkable fact of this conference was that all these States are practically unarmed. Although the meeting made such an impression, it was not on account of the military might it represented; this power was nil. Even the two giant states, China and India, were without military power. However, leaving China apart, as she is still officially without relations with the Western world, India was a country of great power; the fact that she does not plough up the world with her battleships and bombers does not appear to lessen her influence. Moreover, it is sufficient to note the importance that the great world powers attach to the friendship of the Arab countries, which have populations amounting to some millions at least, and which are unprovided with any military force, to see that there is something other than military force which contributes to the importance of nations.

As international relations develop, and as, therefore, countries have more need of each other, so a balance made up of as many elements as possible will be formed, and war, or the threat of war, that is, the military element, will be gradually stifled by a mesh of inter-relationships so involved that no one will be able to extricate themselves.

When the Hungarian revolution broke out in 1956, India demanded that an observer be sent to Budapest. The Russians opposed this move. It must be admitted that they could still do that. Yet that a country like India, at the other end of the world, a country which only twenty years ago was still a British dominion and considered as an inferior, that this country could, in 1956, intervene in Europe and offer to arbitrate, and no one leapt up in indignation, no one burst out laughing; and in addition, that this should be a country entirely without arms, while Russia is one of the two countries which hold all the bombs, surely this heralds the coming of a new world.

It is true that Russia sets much store by the goodwill of India, but this is not for military reasons; and she does not think of employing her own military power against India. No, there is something other than military power.

It is also true that there are armed conflicts, in Asia and in Africa. France has had long and bitter experience of this. However, these conflicts are not wars in the sense of armed conflict between States. Some are more in the nature of revolts, and are the result of the sudden upheaval of colonial situations; others, like the Indonesian conflict, are more in the nature of an internal revolution. These conflicts show that armed forces are necessary to a certain extent; but it is quite a different matter from that of universal conflagration and the use of nuclear weapons.

There remains, therefore, at this moment, a threat of war between the Communist world and the Western world of parliamentary democracies, This threat cannot be done away with all at once; but it is essential to bring to bear on governments who threaten the world sufficient pressure to make it more and more difficult for them to launch such a war.

At the point we find ourselves, the two States who are the principal actors are agreed in declaring that they will not take the initiative, but that they are ready to retaliate, and that they are continuing to pursue their researches in the preparation of more and more destructive weapons. We have also seen that the destructive nature of the weapon can be a motive for not using it, especially if the adversary also possesses it. Moreover, in the last twelve years or so, it has already happened that one of the adversaries possessed a weapon which the other did not have, that they alone possessed it, at least for a few months, and that they did not take advantage of this momentary superiority. This again is a fact. I have said several times that it is essential to take into account all the facts, and that they must be accepted such as they are.

On the other hand, there is a continually growing protest against nuclear experiments throughout the whole world, notably in scientific circles; and this protest is gaining ground from country to country, even in areas very far from the possible centres of combat. It cannot be too strongly supported. It is the duty of all, and of Catholics in particular, to associate themselves with this mounting protest, and it is strongly to be hoped that it will become a tidal wave.

Up till now the influence of this movement has had no noticeable effect: the large States continue to pursue their experiments; States which until now have not manufactured nuclear weapons have begun to make them. The political leaders continue to comply with the hypothesis of a possible war; they continue to regard their countries as threatened. Furthermore, military leaders are now technicians, whose function is to prepare for war, and who fulfil their function without thought of anything else. Movements of opinion seem to come up against a brick wall; but it is difficult to appreciate these things at the time when they occur; later on, with the passing of time, the lines of evolution can be disentangled. For the moment, we know that we must try to stop nuclear experiments of a military character, and all men of goodwill must work to this end.

However, even today, a certain line of evolution can be traced between 1945 and the present time. The threat of total war, which was thought to have completely disappeared at the end of the Second World War, rapidly reappeared, and the threat increased continually until about 1953. Since then it has decreased. In the last few years, negotiations have been constantly renewed with a view to putting an end to the arms race. What is preventing a conclusion being reached is the fact that there is still no mutual trust; but it is obvious to all impartial observers, as we have already noted, that trust can only develop in an atmosphere of collaboration, even though collaboration can only develop in an atmosphere of trust.

This would be a vicious circle if, as many partisans of peace at any price believe, it were necessary to establish total trust all at once. However, there is no need for that. There can exist a state of mitigated trust or mitigated distrust; there are such things as mixed attitudes, and it is not possible to have an absolutely simple attitude towards a man, because man is not a simple being. As far as the question of peace is concerned, it is possible to have an evolution in the sense of a decrease of mistrust and an increase of trust.

A few years ago relationships between the Soviet world and the parliamentary world were renewed and increased. Westerners travelled more easily into Soviet countries and Soviet travellers appeared in Western countries; professors from both worlds met in congresses. All this will not kill the threat of war at one blow, but it is an evolution.

When after this one reads the pontifical documents, it is easy to recognize that they correspond exactly to circumstances, and one understands the appeal that the pope continually makes to Catholics, to play the rôle in the world which their faith requires of them, affirming the duty of mutual aid and giving an example of it.

The Christian attitude is firm, as well as being at the same time realistic and adaptable. It is necessary to be adaptable in order to be realistic, because man is not a simple being. We shall work for peace, less by crying out: "Peace, peace", than by working to develop a spirit of universal mutual aid; the spirit of mutual aid will give rise to mutual aid institutions. In so far as these become more powerful, so the risk of war breaking out will recede.

As regards nuclear discoveries, there is no question of stopping scientific progress, but of guiding it into peaceful uses. If we are to understand the pontifical view in particular, we should bear in mind as we read the texts in which the pope says that a State cannot be forced to disarm while it is not guaranteed against aggression, those texts in which he invites learned men to put themselves at the service of human progress.

Incessantly Pius XII called for agreement. The action of Catholics must be to participate in all those movements which lead to the development of agreement. It is there that they will find that their faith is the purest and most powerful support.

CHAPTER VI

PATRIOTISM AND THE WORLD

To end this review of the whole question we must say in what way the Christian must still keep his patriotic sentiments, and in what way or to what extent these should eventually be adapted to the new situation in the world.

PRESENT TRENDS

The words that we have just read themselves raise a problem: should we still keep our patriotic sentiments? This word "still" will seem blasphemous to some, while others will agree with a student of rhetoric who wrote in reply to an inquiry: "Native land, patriotism, these words no longer have any meaning in this day and age."

In this field, as in every other which concerns the international order, circumstances have evolved with such rapidity that some people have the impression of living in an entirely new world in which we must purely and simply abandon our old ideas, while others cling to these old ideas all the more dearly the more they feel that they are threatened. Patriotism, like all human affections, is a sentiment which becomes noticeable mainly, and sometimes exclusively, when the object of it is threatened. Those people who do not feel that their country is threatened sometimes display very little patriotism. Until very recently this attitude was fairly characteristic of the Anglo-Saxon countries, where there was an innate feeling of security. Spectacular demonstrations of patriotism were considered in bad taste. In a community that is taken for granted, the members of the community will criticize it quite freely. When it is in danger, the smallest criticism appears to be treason; this can be seen in families as well as in nations.

Consequently there arise at the moment various different reactions, which give the impression of confusion. On the one hand, a certain number of people, especially among the young, are growing angry because the international community, which the whole world recognizes as necessary, has not yet been constituted. They feel that it is the old countries which are holding everything up. Hence we get the reaction of the German who refused to register his child except as a citizen of the world, and that of Garry Davis, who tried to travel freely in every country, on the grounds that frontiers and passports were outdated.

On the other hand, in the international organizations, no one has succeeded in eliminating the absolute autonomy of States, and a great many who would like to see this achieved react violently when others try to interfere in the affairs of their own countries. The French have experienced this most painfully during the Suez and Algerian incidents. However, India's attitude over Kashmir is the same. Yet the Indian leaders are among those who serenely support the most international ideas.

This confusion of which we are speaking is nowhere more forcibly illustrated than in the new States which have been constituted since the war in Asia and Africa. We find on the one hand a national hypersensitivity, which makes them obsessed with maintaining their independence in every sphere, even if they are incapable of using it, and gives them a mistrust of all foreigners, especially Europeans, who formerly dominated them, and on the other hand we find an international sense, which is illustrated by their relations between each other, of which the conferences at Bandung and Accra are examples. These peoples who have so recently attained independence, are ready to adapt themselves to the necessity of international collaboration which now exists, but they distrust those nations to which only yesterday they belonged as colonies. Such people may thus oscillate between nationalism and internationalism according to the company they are in.

THE ORIGIN OF THESE TRENDS

These trends arise in the main from the French Revolution, and from all the similar movements which it provoked throughout the world. These movements had been smouldering for a long time, and historians can find many earlier examples of them, but it was the French Revolution which set the trend for contemporary times, on the ideological level.

Thus has developed the idea of the National State, that is, the idea that the State is an institution which gives the national group its finished form and its accomplishment, and thus has begun the movement of nationalities, by which the different national communities aim at forming a State. Italian unity and German unity represent the two summits of the movement of the nineteenth century, and after the 1914 war, the victorious powers proclaimed, at the instigation of President Wilson, the right of small peoples to decide for themselves. The inter-war period is the great era of nationalism, the right of the nation being established absolutely and national egoism being unreservedly asserted.

However, also since the nineteenth century, as the development of communications has increased contacts among peoples, so this has led to the development of international agreement. Innumerable international agreements were entered into concerning the postal, telegraph and railway services, and authors' rights. In the scientific world, a truly international scientific atmosphere was established, and scientists from all over the world worked in collaboration. At the end of the century peace conferences sought to codify the laws of war, which would limit its ravages, and, after the First World War, the League of Nations was set up, with a view to making a definite end to wars and organizing international mutual aid in conformity with the needs of international welfare.

The League of Nations for a few years was looked upon with high hope, but it came up against relentless opposition from all conservative centres which, under the pretext of defending patriotism, developed a radical nationalism. The nationalist reaction reached its height, first in Italy, with Fascism, then in Germany, with Nazism. These reactions on the international level went together with the political movements, internationalism being related to parliamentary democracy, and nationalism to authoritarian government. In France, the nationalist movement, embodied in the Action Française, was at the same time fighting parliamentary democracy.

The twenty years of the inter-war period were a time of intellectual fermentation, and of extremely lively emotional developments. Among others, in the legal field, an important study movement grew up to analyse the ideas pertaining to the independence of States.

At the same time, since the nineteenth century, there developed a sentimental international movement aiming at overcoming frontiers in order to unite the whole human race; and this movement was generally linked to advanced political movements, such as socialism and anarchism. According to Karl Marx, the native land was an invention of the exploiting capitalists, who hoped in this way to make the proletariat accept the exploitation of which they were the victims, and the socialist movements were preparing to bring down all national barriers. When the 1914 war began to threaten, it was hoped that the socialists would render it impossible, by proclaiming the solidarity of the workers over and above all frontiers, and one of the great disillusions of the time was to see them range themselves everywhere in line with middle-class patriotism.

However, all these setbacks developed, in a certain number of honest men, a reaction against the obstacles in the way of agreement, and this reaction continually engenders all kinds of movements for peace and for the constitution of a society over and above national limitations. Those who militate in this direction are often idealists, driven by strong feelings; and they often react violently against the immobility of those who defend positions limited by their immediate horizons. Thus for nearly a century the same resolutions have been repeatedly urged. Sometimes it seems that no progress has been made, and yet, the close observer will notice that the question has gradually become clearer, and that we have now arrived at the moment when something can be done.

MY NATIVE LAND AND MY COUNTRY

My country. . . . Man naturally loves his country. Love of country is linked to the legitimate attachment of man to the mission that he has to fulfil on earth. We have something to do on earth, and to accomplish our work we must develop. No one knows this better than the Christian, for he knows that it is God who put him on this earth and that he is here to give glory to God.

However, man attains his full development through the influences to which he is subject, his family, his milieu—all the milieus in which he lives—his country. He has an affection for all which relates to his personal development, both things and people.

It is therefore evident that affection for one's country does not arise solely from people but from things, from the countryside, from the mountains or the plains, the sea or the woods, the village, the district, the language, everything which goes to make up the environment in which one grows up, and which unites one to those who are of the same environment at the same time as it distinguishes one from others.

I use the word "distinguish" here. Patriotism becomes unhealthy when it does not limit itself to distinguishing, but goes on to separate or oppose. This is often the case. This brings in the question of morality. Affection for one's country becomes contempt of others as soon as man becomes proud. National pride is one of the plagues of humanity. Each nation tends to think of itself as a race of supermen. How can human unity be achieved with nations who each believe that they are the élite, destined to dominate the others?

However, this sentiment can be mitigated, even if it does not disappear altogether. It can be sufficiently mitigated for collaboration to be made possible. This is a common experience. Regional loyalty may seem to prevail over loyalty to the country as a whole; a man of one region is convinced of his superiority over the rest of the country, and it has been asserted that it was the group to which the speaker belonged which made up the true value of the country—that it was thanks to his group, for example, that they won the war. However, this feeling is sufficiently subdued for it to be dominated by an affection for the whole of the country, the great communal homeland for which one's own little homeland would, if necessary, be sacrificed.

Great or little homeland: man has not just one homeland, but several. My homeland is my country; but the term "my country" covers several entities. The country of my birth may be England or the United States, but it may also be Yorkshire or Virginia, London or Chicago, and none excludes the others. I can only be an Englishman or

an American by living in one district of England or the
U.S.A., and I can only belong to a district by living in one
place in that district.

The linguistic use of the word "country" as a synonym
of "village" is a good illustration of this variety of mean-
ings. For "my country" is also "my homeland". Though
"my country" may be the village where I was born, that
does not prevent England or the U.S.A. being "my
country", and all the country is "my homeland".

The word "homeland", like the word "country" is used
to mean any human or geographical environment to which
the personality is linked.

Man has therefore several degrees of homeland, usually
coordinated, and homeland is usually taken to mean that
community for which one has a particular community
feeling. Normally speaking, all community feelings are
coordinated and have varying degrees. When coordination
is not spontaneous, when some men experience an affection
towards two opposing groups, or when they think they
have duties towards two groups which appear incompatible,
they feel torn, and this engenders social troubles. This is
the case with nationalist movements within the State. Members of the national group have the impression that affection for the State is in opposition to affection for the nation.
This may end in civil war, or may simply cause uneasiness.

Little or great homeland: these are extremely variable
ideas. The idea of a great homeland does not seem to
have acquired the deep roots or the durability that we have
known it to have, until the nineteenth century when it
developed through the principle of nationalism and the
concentration of community feeling upon the State. In the
Middle Ages, Christianity formed a republic of peoples,
who often fought against each other because they were
barbarians, but who at the same time had the feeling of
forming a community. When St Albert the Great, who
was Rhenish, and St Thomas, who was a Neapolitan, taught

at Paris, they had little impression of being abroad. This continued up to the eighteenth century, as can be seen by the travels of Voltaire, or by the number of Germans who lived in France, such as Holbach or Marshal Saxe.

This fixation of the idea of the State being the great homeland has something rather artificial about it. It seems natural to a Frenchman, but the Duchy of Luxembourg has 300,000 inhabitants, and is the size of one department of France. Yet what homeland could these inhabitants have outside Luxembourg? And there are many States of only one million inhabitants or even less, in Central America and in the Near East.

Until fairly recently, the homeland was a spontaneous idea; the homeland was the community with which one felt identified. When, in the Middle Ages, the Bretons or the Flemish fought the King of France, who was their suzerain, they never thought of themselves as traitors, any more than did the burghers of Bruges when they rebelled against the Count of Flanders. However, in the nineteenth century the idea of the homeland hardened into being that of the State, and nationalism has consisted in trying to arrest it at this stage.

PRACTICAL DUTY

Man must love his homeland, because he must love everything which allows him to accomplish his mission. He must love his homeland, all his homelands, small and great, each in its place, each in accordance with the extent to which it helps him to be himself.

There is therefore no natural difference between the various forms of homeland. The homeland is a reality, the reality of human and geographical environment, which allows man to fulfil himself.

Here again, the French Revolution proves to be a decisive date; and its action in this field is linked to the ideological whole which dominates it. It was founded on an individualistic idea of democracy, conceived in the form of a State which would be the sole link between individuals. As well as being the sole link between individuals, the State was the emanation of the community of individuals. The polling booth was, in a way, its symbol. The State sprang up from the votes of the electors, and this vote was decided upon in the isolation of the polling booth, where each individual would find himself alone with his conscience. All private groups were suppressed. Here again, we find a symbol of the system in the suppression of provinces, which were replaced by departments with arbitrary names and areas. It was essential that the French should have nothing which resembled a homeland apart from the State. This idea foundered upon reality, for men form groups outside the State. They form them spontaneously, inevitably. After more than a century and a half, the provinces still subsist in France; but the continuity of the departmental system has had as an effect that the departments themselves have also gradually acquired a moral reality, that is, a place in people's minds.

The two tendencies are constantly in opposition, and periodically they clash: there is the unitarian, state socialist, authoritarian tendency, that is to be found especially in authoritarian states. This is the "All in the state, by the state, for the state" of Mussolini. Then there is the federational tendency which is truly democratic, which is seeking a political organization, and supports movements of social reality.

We must love all the communities to which we are linked, for the good that they bring us, and we must collaborate in their development, so that they may continue to exercise their beneficial action on their members. The duty of patriotism is the duty of collaboration.

If God allows me to be born in such and such an environment, it is because my work as a man is to be accomplished under the conditions of that environment. If, for example, I am born into a nation of black Africans which historical circumstances have, until just recently, held back from the general civilization of the world, I inherit from the people among whom I was born and among whom I grew up, a whole mass of characteristics which make it inevitable that I shall develop better and act more usefully by devoting the resources of my personality to those people, and it is among those people that I shall best accomplish my task as a man.

Maurras once defined the homeland as "a hereditary advance". This was because he was French, and was convinced that France was the first country of the world. But there are homelands which are "hereditary setbacks". A certain number of young coloured men who are studying in France do not want to return to their countries, because they have precisely this feeling that their country is a hereditary setback to them. However, they can take back to their country something which will enable it to develop, although they can add nothing to France. Born in their own country, endowed with the character and sensitivity of their race, familiar with the population, their mother tongue being the language of their country, they are fitted to act in their country in a way that they are not fitted to act in France. This also explains why, throughout history, exile has been considered as a misfortune. In the literature of every nation there are poems expressing the pain of exile, as well as the joy of those who return to their country after a long absence. All this is human, natural and true. It has a ring of human authenticity, and will last for ever.

I know very well that there are other reasons for emigrating, and that one may be called upon to emigrate further than from one district to another in one's own country; but the case just quoted is a simple one, showing why, normally speaking, the place of each one is in his own country.

Let each one stay in his own place; let each one work
in his own place at the common task of men; let each
nation work in its place, and the human race will achieve
the order which it is called upon to bring about.

THE GREAT HÙMAN HOMELAND

I have just said: "the common task of men". But these
very words extend thought beyond homelands—beyond
what are called homelands.

How can the Christian be unaware of this overstepping
of historical frontiers, if he truly understands the meaning
of Christian brotherhood?

I have already touched on this matter; but the present
contingency forces me to explain in detail the nature of
patriotic sentiment because, in our day and age, we find
ourselves at a new stage in human history, which calls to
mind the situation at the end of the Middle Ages.

At that time regional patriotism, that of lordships and
communes, had given way to national patriotism, that of
the great States. This was a gradual movement, which
suffered many setbacks, and it was not completely finished
by the end of the *ancien régime*. But today, the new stage
has come upon us rapidly, and world order must be
achieved without delay, or catastrophes will arise, and it
must be achieved institutionally before it can be achieved
effectively.

The formula we have just read may appear mysterious
to some; but we need only compare the situation with the
former stage to understand. When European States, with
France in the lead, began to take consistent outlines about
the sixteenth century, this unification of the State went
hand in hand with the assertion of royal power, and when
patriotic sentiment was directed with all its force on the
country, it was directed towards a reality, towards an
"existing fact". The assertion of French patriotism is often

dated from the Hundred Years War, and the coming together of the hearts of men, of which Joan of Arc was the
final expression. Today it is essential that Europe for the
Europeans, the universe for all men, should become a
homeland also, that is, that Europeans should become
aware that Europe is, to a certain extent, their country;
and that men should become aware that the world, to a
certain extent, is their country. Now neither Europe nor
the world exists as yet as an organized community. At the
end of the Middle Ages, the States existed as organized
communities, and the problem was simply to assert this
fact. Today it is painfully obvious in negotiations concerning Europe, and in those taking place in the United
Nations, that the difficulty arises from the fact that everyone is aware of what the times require, and understands
the necessity and urgency of unity, but that this does not
present itself as an existing reality that can be loved.

A comparison with the family will help to illustrate this.
One of the reasons for the limitation of births is that
parents only love their children when they exist. It often
happens that parents do not, or no longer want to have
children; and yet if they have another child in spite of
this, they love the baby from the day it is born. Thus
forethought is a source of the fall in the birth-rate. The
child who does not exist is an abstraction; love is a
fundamental essential; it is directed towards existing things.
While the child is unborn what does exist, for example, are
the facilities of life which will be decreased if a baby
arrives. We are attached to what we have. Yet once the
child has come, and it is loved, we are ready to make the
sacrifices which its presence imposes on us.

It is the same with the homeland. Once Europe has come,
once the world has come, they will be loved. The difficulty
is to find the starting point, that is, to give them sufficient
consistency for sentiment to be directed towards them.

As I write these lines, a small Europe is being painfully hewn out by six countries, and it has not yet succeeded in establishing a political order. It is a little thing compared with the needs of the times. However, freedom of movement has been achieved between these six countries, and if human contacts increase to the extent that the inhabitants forget the meaning of the frontier, in fifty years' time, or maybe less, we shall see the birth of European patriotism.

Must we then abandon what up till now has been known as patriotism? The question itself is the punishment for patriotic exclusivity which has continually developed during the last two centuries, concentrating all feelings of communal affection on the nation or on the State, one group joining the other because, by virtue of the principle of nationalities, a national group does not reach completion until it forms a State—*ein Volk, ein Staat*, as the Germans say—and the result is that the State fights all individualities within itself, because it cannot allow several nationalities in one State. The State, identified with the nation, was therefore the sole object of community affection. I am using here a somewhat unusual term because homeland and patriotism are so closely identified with the State, that it has become difficult to use the term patriotism in any sense other than affection for the State, without embarking on long explanations.

This also explains the reaction of present-day youth, who say that we must abandon the idea of homeland, that it is nothing but an anachronism. They react against patriotism in the form in which it is put to them by those who claim to be its authentic representatives.

In actual fact we must love all communities to which we are attached, each in its place and degree. Moreover, communities need each other, as individuals do; national life impregnates regional and local life, as does professional life; today international life impregnates national life. I must have European and world patriotism so that my country may develop to the full, in the same way that my town or my village will only develop fully in an atmosphere of national prosperity.

Indeed, in the very numerous documents in which the popes dealt with the question since the First World War, they habitually reacted against nationalism, and insisted on the idea that international agreements did not interfere with the legitimate rights of nations. As early as 1939, in *Summi Pontificatus*, Pius XII said:

> It is well to insist here that this sense of universal brother-hood, which Christian teaching awakes and keeps alive in our minds, is not opposed to the love of a man's country and of the glorious memories it has for him. It does not forbid a man to work for the promotion of his country's prosperity and of the advantages which it lawfully enjoys. This same Christian teaching assures us that God has established an order of charity which binds us to love better and to cherish more those who are bound to us by special ties.

I do not think there is any need to add to this quotation. The question is simple. What makes it obscure are the exclusive sentiments which have been over-excited. From this point of view, what is called today the federal tendency is preparing minds to extricate themselves from the block-age of sentiments centred on the nation or on the State. To admit, within States, as many centres of affection as there are groups of interests and centres of life, is preparing to understand that we can have, and should have in our day and age, centres of life over and above the State. These centres can only be constituted if men understand their reason for being, and desire that they should exist.

It is said that necessity is the mother of invention. We are today faced with a vital necessity; but it must be satis-fied through an organization which has already been invented, and which was not designed for it, and the old organization resists any new organization which seeks to break in.

THE CIRCLE OF NATIONS

I must love all men, because they are my brothers, and I must love my country because it is the providential place where I can use the gifts I have received from God in order to work for the welfare of the human race.

I do not directly influence the human race; I only influence it through the intermediary of my country, and together with my people, my compatriots, I must work in order to put my nation at the service of the human race. My country will attain all the grandeur of which it is capable if it brings to the human race all it is able to bring, and if, through that, the human race possesses a form of beauty that it would not otherwise have had.

Men have a task to accomplish together; it is to develop all forms of human activity in such a way as to make the whole life of the human race a hymn to the Creator. If we bear this principle in mind, and if we look at the world, we see that there is still a large part of the human race whose life is in no way a hymn to the Creator, for example, all the peoples suffering from malnutrition, tormented by disease, and even in the most highly developed countries, the numerous cankers of disorganized families, deformed children, and the poverty-stricken, under-nourished, badly-clothed, miserably-housed classes. Yet the world today has one gleam of hope, because civilization offers the means of averting these scourges.

Yet there is one condition: that is that we must agree among ourselves and work together, the community must include the whole world, so that each one will feel himself implicated in the happiness and misfortune of others; and the others are not just those who belong to the same local or national community, but those who belong to the world community.

No particular community should be suppressed. In the same way as individual groups should be allowed to exist within the nation, so nations should be allowed to exist in the universal plan. Union is not uniformity, and the very word coordination implies that the whole is made up of various elements. Variety will remain; each people, each group, has its own bent; each has its own centres of affection; each must develop according to its capabilities; each must bring to the human race the values which it alone possesses.

> And as nations become more civilized, they become more highly differentiated in their ways of life and of managing their affairs. That is no reason why they should renounce the unity of the human family. Rather, they should enrich that family by making their own contribution to its variety, according to their several endowments. They should exchange, mutually, the advantages they enjoy (Pius XII, *Summi Pontificatus*).

Even in limited communities, each part has its own life and originality. We know that States have too often tended to scoff at individualities, on the pretext of safeguarding unity, and that, for their part, the individualities have easily tended towards exclusivity and separatism. All these problems can be found in national history; but today they have arisen on the world scale.

Men who have today passed the age of maturity have been formed during the course of two wars, and on account of these two wars, by an exclusive patriotism exacerbated by necessity. During the war the problem was to save one's country, and to urge men to make sacrifices for the safety of their country. Consequently, emphasis was laid on this aspect, and men came out of the war filled with a national patriotism which would brook no limitation.

Already, however, the war had reached a world scale, and the fate of a country in Europe, for example, depended on results in the Pacific as well as on the Channel coasts. But as many Europeans had no occasion to fight in the Pacific, they could only interest themselves in their own country, and the situation itself concentrated their thought on their own country. But once the war was ended European and world needs were revealed with disconcerting rapidity. For men over a certain age this entailed a complete change of attitude. Age makes it more and more difficult to change one's attitude. At fifty a man does not have the flexibility he had at twenty.

It is impossible not to admire these older men who placed themselves at the forefront of the movement. In particular, the European movement will always be linked with the name of Schumann; and this German-sounding name, which is the name of a Frenchman, is symbolic of the removal of barriers by its very sound. Nevertheless it is essential that public opinion should support this symbol.

We have said, the circle of nations; the agreement of different characteristics. They do not oppose, rather they complement each other; but they must be understood, and to understand it is essential not to stop at contemplating one's own qualities and those of one's people.

There must be no separation, still less opposition, between one's own interests and the common good, for it is in everyone's interest that all as a whole should develop. It is in our interest that Indians should be Indians, Chinese should be Chinese, Colombians should be Colombians, etc., so that each can contribute its own harmony in the concert of the human race. The human race will not achieve full development unless every nation and every race brings to the collective work the values which belong to them alone; and if our homeland develops within a more ordered human race it will also develop more harmoniously.

But this requires a spirit of friendship one to another. We must, so to speak, accept and expect in advance that others should be different from us, and should possess values that we lack. This implies—we find ourselves back to the same problem—that we should not close in upon ourselves, thinking that only our own values are authentic, contemptuous of all which in others differs from ourselves.

It is well known that this exclusiveness is very character-istic of the primitive races. Formerly the Eskimos, whose only contact with Europeans was with the English, had a proverb: "As stupid as an Englishman." They despised the English, who did not even know how to make a harpoon! Are there not many among us who are still at the same stage as those Eskimos?

My brother, the foreigner. There must be a spirit of friendship towards our brothers. We must welcome them or go to them sympathetically, glad not only to be in agreement on points where collaboration is necessary, but glad also to find them different, to have something to learn from them. Primitive peoples, under-developed peoples, think they have nothing to learn from anyone. . . . It is also undoubtedly a sign of under-development to think that one has everything to give and nothing to receive.

At international meetings it often happens that Ameri-cans and Europeans give offence, without meaning to, to the Far Eastern peoples, by their naïve condescension, ex-pressed by a charitably inspired desire to come to the aid of the under-developed countries, while these countries are aware that they can give something of value that the former do not even suspect. But this value is of quite an-other order. . . . Already our old Europe has had some experience of this. The French sometimes react violently against the Americans, when the latter show their pity for the material difficulties of France, and offer their aid without appearing to be aware that France possesses other values.

The remedy for these national susceptibilities which fester, and for these forms of national sufficiency, will only be found in a spirit of friendship for one another. It requires a complete moral education. At the present time work on this is going on all over the world, especially in youth movements.

A certain number of informed minds, in leading circles, are in the forefront of the movement. They are to be found in governments, in political assemblies; they are found among writers, publishers and journalists; they are found in business circles, and among the clergy, and we have noted how insistently Pius XII constantly returned to the matter. There are workers on all sides.

In this way evidence of universal fraternity will be amassed. Gradually the idea will emerge that each one must make his contribution to the common task. Gradually the idea will emerge that the common task is incumbent upon all, and that this work is directed towards the construction of a world in which life will offer to all the means of developing as human beings.

Each time something has to be achieved, one comes up against the obstacle of national egoisms, each nation desiring that only the others should make sacrifices. We cannot wait for these individualisms to disappear all at once. It is the same as the question of war; they can only fade away gradually: and, in the assemblies, the leaders of each country must defend as well as they can the national interests which they represent. But, little by little, in everyone's conscience, awareness of the need for agreement, common to all, the need for agreement, mutual aid, coordination, legal order and common authority for controlling ·communal action, will increase.

For the first time since men appeared on earth, they hold in their hands the means of establishing a universal community, and the development of civilization, the improvement of the standard of living of the human race, of all peoples and of each people, will be the reward. As Pius XII said, who better than the Christian is prepared, by his whole education, for this work?

The circle of nations and patriotism: if I love my country I must want it to cooperate, and to be the first to cooperate in the work which will bring about the welfare of the human race; if I love my country, I must desire that it should develop within the human race as a whole, where it will meet with other nations, who will stand shoulder to shoulder with it to accomplish the great work of universal civilization. If I love the human race, I shall desire my country to play its part in the concert; but, as the musician who plays his instrument in an orchestra wants his instrument to be perfect, and must try to play his part perfectly, so my country will find its true worth by contributing to the human race all that it is capable of, and it will benefit from all that the human race achieves.

The homeland and the world: one in the other, one for the others.

CONCLUSION

In the preceding pages I have tried to define the position of the Christian in relation to the international integration of the world. At the point we have reached today, the human race will be arrested in its development unless it establishes a society which will cover the whole world; and any halt will very shortly bring about retrogression. Moreover, it is now possible to bring about this universal integration of society; technically speaking, that is, materially speaking, it does not even present any great difficulties. To make contact between Paris and New Delhi is easier today, materially speaking, than it was to make contact between Paris and Marseilles in the days of Louis XIV. The difficulties are psychological and moral.

The psychological difficulties arise from a lack of formation and information of minds; the moral difficulties arise, fundamentally, from the fact that men are centred upon themselves. It is here that Christians have a decisive rôle to play.

The moral question involves the psychological question, for if one loves one's neighbour, one is interested in him.

The Church gives the example. She has always been concerned with universality. She was unable to fulfil immediately the commandment she received from the Saviour, "Go forth and preach to all nations", because not all nations were accessible to her. It was a problem of a material nature. But, each time a country or a continent was open to the propagation of the faith, missionaries went there with great enthusiasm, and missionary history is full of heroic imprudences as well as overflowing love.

In our days also, the Church loudly asserts the profound meaning of the universality which she still possesses, and the profound meaning of fundamental brotherhood and equality of races, peoples and men. No one can attend an international meeting of Catholics without becoming aware of the atmosphere of brotherhood which is so obviously present. And we know that the Church was concerned with taking root in Asia and Africa at a time when States thought only of exploiting them. We cannot recount this history here; it began with the apostles and continues throughout the centuries in the midst of a thousand contradictions.

This task at which, in fact, the Church has laboured alone in the past, must today be achieved by the entire human race on the temporal plane. As Pius XII said in a passage already quoted, Christians are especially prepared to associate themselves with it, and even to exercise an influence which may prove to be decisive. But if this is to be achieved they must be true Christians.

Now we have seen what is meant by the word Christian. There are several different degrees of Christians, and active Christians are only a limited number. The pope teaches; the bishops repeat what he has said, and the Christian masses listen with half an ear. The pontifical and episcopal words sometimes have more effect in certain circles of unbelievers than in Christian circles.

For some years episcopal as well as pontifical documents on the international question, on the duty of mutual aid, the correct idea of patriotism and the attitude of the Christian towards war have continually increased. They follow events, for, as we have said, the teachings of the hierarchy are acts. They are acts of government, a government which is not limited to theoretical teaching, but which teaches in order to direct action. The problem, or the whole mass of problems which are to the fore, are those which concern Africa; the teachings of the hierarchy on this matter are innumerable.

As regards the unity of Christianity and the world, the question of the rôle of Catholics in the international integration of the world is essentially that of an active minority. Groups must be formed, such as are sometimes called "shock groups" today, as numerous and as active as possible, which will spread the idea of universal brotherhood not only in Catholic circles, but throughout the world, recruiting collaborators wherever they succeed in arousing interest, ready to join international organizations and to put themselves at the service of the common cause of the human race wherever there is an opportunity.

Like all human affairs, the life of the Church is, above all, ruled by an active minority. In the history of humanity, nothing is ever done by the masses, and even when events appear to have been provoked by the uprising of the masses, these uprisings have resulted from movements prepared by a small number. In particular, in our time, the profound transformations of human life, those which result from the movement of ideas, like liberalism, Communism, dechristianization or Christian renewal, and those which directly transform material life, like the scientific movement, arise from a small number of men. In the Church also, a small number pledge themselves to achieve the Christian ideal in their own life, and to lead others to it, and these are the ones which make the life of the Church. The masses evolve slowly and to the extent to which they are influenced by these few.

It is asked: "Are Christians capable of playing in the world the rôle of leaven to which the Saviour has called them?" The answer depends on whether the "little flock" will be numerous and active enough. In the nineteenth century it was not, and consequently there appeared excessive nationalism and wars. Today one has the impression, in the Church, of a great armed vigil. Everywhere there are signs of an awakening of conscience. The future will tell us whether we shall arrive in time.

To conclude, it will be of use to recall once again that the life of the Church, that is, Christian life, is the life of God in men, and that this life of God is brought to us through the mediation of Christ. The problem of the Church is, above all, to raise in the world the level of the divine life, which is called grace, and it is raised in the world by being raised in souls. In proportion to the extent to which the level of grace rises, divine action becomes more intense in men, and through them, in the world; to this extent will the spirit of Christ penetrate more deeply into humanity, and the spirit of Christ is, above all, charity, this fraternal charity without which there can be no profound agreement among men.

The problem of the participation of the Christian in the organization of the universal society is therefore linked to the fact that the Christian should be an authentic Christian, that is, that he should live through the life which Christ brings to him. To the extent to which he does this, he will react in a Christlike manner, and he will work effectively to achieve an increase of love among men.

Catholics today, in the development of international life, have a greater place than they had fifty years ago. This is essential to the development of divine life which is manifested in the Church in all its most varied aspects. It must never be forgotten that the Church forms a whole and that Christianity is life. Christ is the Saviour, and he teaches in order to show the way to salvation. The international doctrine cannot be treated as a purely intellectual doctrine, to be developed as a theory without regard to practical consequences. The doctrine is grounded in action. The reality of Christianity, the reality of the Church, is not to be a school where a perfect doctrine is taught, but to save. One essential aspect of salvation today is to succeed in establishing a worldwide organization of the human race, and this organization cannot be uniquely the work of Christians. But it is in the contribution that they make to it, and in the influence that they exercise, that Christians will show that they possess the formula of life.

SELECT BIBLIOGRAPHY

In this series: BOVIS, André de, S.J.: *The Church: Christ's Mystery and Sacrament*; HOLLIS, Christopher: *The Church and Economics* (American edn, *Christianity and Economics*); RÉTIF, Louis and André: *The Mission of the Church in the World*.

DANIÉLOU, J., S.J.: *The Salvation of the Nations*, London and New York, Sheed and Ward, 1949.

FREMANTLE, Anne (Editor): *The Papal Encyclicals in Their Historical Context*, New York, New American Library of World Literature, 1956.

GURIAN, W., and FITZSIMMONS, M. A.: *The Catholic Church in World Affairs*, Oxford, Blackwell, and Indiana, Notre Dame Univ. Press, 1954.

HAWKINS, D. B. J.: *Man and Morals*, London and New York, Sheed and Ward, 1960.

HUGHES, Philip: *The Pope's New Order: A Systematic Study of the Social Encyclicals and Addresses from Leo XIII to Pius XII*, London, Burns and Oates, 1943.

JOURNET, Charles: *The Church of the Word Incarnate*, London and New York, Sheed and Ward, 1955.

LUBAC, Henri de, S.J.: *Catholicism, A Study of Dogma in Relation to the Corporate Destiny of Mankind*, translated by Lancelot C. Sheppard, London, Burns and Oates, and New York, Sheed and Ward, 1950.

MARITAIN, Jacques: *Man and the State*, London, Hollis and Carter, 1954, and Chicago, Univ. of Chicago Press, 1955.

WILLIAMS, M. J.: *Catholic Social Thought*, New York, Ronald Press, 1954.

WYNNE, John: *The Great Encyclical Letters of Leo XIII*, New York, Benziger, 1903.